Taking it to the Streets

Prophetic Evangelism

By
Greg DeVries

ISBN: 1494921774
ISBN 13: 9781494921774
Library of Congress Control Number: 2014900403
CreateSpace Independent Publishing Platform
North Charleston, South Carolina

Dedication

This book is solely dedicated to the One who made it all happen, The Holy Spirit of God. And to all those it has not yet happened to, those who have yet to hear the good news of Jesus Christ.

Table of Contents

Endorsements

I believe every word in this book to be truth. Not only because I have heard these stories, but I have seen most of them take place with my own eyes. I believe this to be a powerful ministry tool that anyone wanting to grow in faith should get his or her hands on!

Spencer DeVries
Worship and Youth Pastor
The Rock Family Worship Center
Scottsboro, AL

In the pages of Taking It to the Streets you will find wisdom, insight, and inspiration that will challenge and equip you to fulfill Christ's Great Commission right on your own doorstep. Your heart will be stirred to action as Greg DeVries shares treasure with you from many years of front line ministry in the cities of America and around the world. I've had the privilege of knowing and walking with Greg as a friend and coworker for over twenty years. He loves God, he loves people, and he is actively involved "Taking It to the Streets"

Ken Pounders
Missionary Evangelist
Priority! Evangelism.

More than words creating a buzz about the latest greatest fad in evangelism or the prophetic, the content between the covers of this book challenge us to buzz around the Word. I can hear Greg saying, "Don't let this just be a resource, but let it connect you to the Source." Glean from these stories, and let them sharpen your ears to hear the Spirit speaking to our generation. I am confident of this: No greater joy would Greg have than knowing that we, the body of Christ, walk in the way of truth with the presence of the Spirit sharing with others the heart of the Father revealed through and by Jesus. May these words; these stories move us to yield our lives to God for the redemption of the times in which we live!

Whitney Mitchell
Pastor 1ˢᵗ UMC
Waynesboro, TN

There are very few people I know like my brother Greg DeVries. He hears from God, steps out in simple faith and then sees God do amazing things. It's as if the stories of the New Testament have been brought to life in the 21st Century, and it's not just in the confines of a church building either, but out on the streets! It's truly remarkable. I've known Greg for many years and he lives and breathes exactly what he preaches. He's the real deal. There's no question in my mind you'll be inspired and challenged in your own walk with God as you read the stories from this book.

Peter Warren
Southwest USA Regional Director
Youth With A Mission

It's about time. As I have heard about these divine appointments for the last 20 years, all I can say is, it's about time that Greg has decided to allow the richness and the mercies of Gods prophetic evangelism to be shared with the Body of Christ. I only hope that it will enrich your life and ministry as much as it has mine.

Don Tomei
Sr. Pastor Restoration Church
Naples Fl.

To understand any subject one must go to someone both gifted and seasoned. Greg Devries is the "go to guy" on Spirit-led evangelism. Greg's strong prophetic anointing combined with his depth of first-hand experiences over many years makes his writing a lethal dose to the gates of hell. Taking It To The Streets is the heartbeat of God! The stories illustrate the means of witnessing for Jesus while the insights reveal the right way to effectively reach this generation with the Gospel of Christ.

I highly recommend this book as a gold mine of understanding the call to be fishers of men and recapture the mission to seek and save, that which was lost!

Pastor Bill Davis,
Pastor, Church of the Shoals
Florence, Alabama

"Greg DeVries is one of my greatest friends in the world. He's the real deal! He lives what he writes and preaches about and has the unique ability to encourage and challenge us all at the

same time. His love for God and the lost is a rare find today. You will be stirred to action by the stories in this book!"
Jay Haizlip
Senior Pastor
The Sanctuary HB
Westminster, CA

My friend, Greg DeVries has a great passion to reach people with the message that really matters...the gospel of Jesus Christ. On the streets of cities across America he has not only been a carrier of Good News but has influenced many to do the same. You will want to read this book and be inspired to reach your world.

Scott Hinkle
Evangelist
Scott Hinkle Outreach Ministries

Foreword

This book has been a long time coming! Greg and I have lived a very exciting and favored life together in the Kingdom of God. It is a blessing to be writing the foreword to this book and to have the privilege to be a part of the dream of seeing this book published and now in your hands. Over the years God has taught us a great many lessons through evangelism. We have met some precious people that are still a part of our lives even today. I'm so glad I have gotten to live with a man of God that is passionate for The Word, the body of Christ, and the lost. Our family has gotten to be an intricate part of ministry in so many facets over the years. I am blessed that our children have seen God move, heard God speak, and experience "God" moments that have forever changed their lives. As you dive into these stories, allow The Lord to ignite a fire in your heart like never before for everyday life to become supernatural. Ask Him for ears to hear, eyes to see, and a heart to obey and follow hard after Him... It reminds me of the old hymn, "Where He leads me I will follow...I'll go with Him, with Him, all the way." Ask Him to lead you, teach you, mold you, and send you....The fields are white unto harvest. God has been so faithful to show up when we step out. He continues to reveal Himself by allowing us to have a part in "taking it to the streets" as you will read in the pages of this book. I have had the great joy and honor of being on some of these encounters you will read about in these pages. What a blessing to serve the Living God and to watch Him move, speak, and change people's lives. I am completely overwhelmed that Greg and I get to walk out this journey called life together. He has been my best friend, my teacher, my encourager, and my great example of what it looks like to walk in the Spirit and obey God no matter what. You will be blessed as you read these **real** stories that happened to **real** people that encountered the **Real** GOD!!

Gretchen DeVries

Preface

Once again, the old saying, "Never say never," has prevailed. I remember saying I would never write a book! I was sincerely concerned that it would be done out of the impulse to gain notoriety or prosperity or just to say, "I did it." As a matter of fact, I really felt that it was the Lord making that impression upon me. Well, come to think of it, I still believe that it was Him making such an impression upon my heart. However, that was Him then, and this book is a result of Him, now!

It seems like yesterday when I heard Him say, "I want you to write a book of stories relating to prophetic evangelism." Believe me, it was not yesterday. I wrestled for years, not wanting to go against my convictions to "never write a book," until He spoke to my heart, saying, "Some things I have you die to so you can live, and other things I have you die to so I can resurrect them and cause others to live." Quickly I was reminded of the Lord speaking to Peter while Peter was in a trance on the rooftop. Peter was in no way going to eat anything that was unclean. He probably felt as though he was being tested, and he was not going to give in. Then he, too, realized that was then and this is now!

The format of this book is very simple. The first and last chapters are bookends containing brief insights pertaining to prophetic evangelism. Each chapter in between consists of short stories that are actual testimonies of prophetic evangelism in the streets. There is real power not only in the spoken word but also in the written word. As it is stated in Revelation 19:10, "The testimony of Jesus is the spirit of prophecy."

My desire is that these testimonies will be a prophetic message to you, enabling you to rise to the calling and stirring of a prophetic generation who takes it to the streets! We overcome the enemy by the blood of the Lamb and the word of our testimony, and by loving not our lives unto death. Please know that the content of this book is not about lifting me up. I think maybe I waited so long to write it to make sure I did not love my life unto death. This is truly for the honor of Him who sent me to do His works and for the encouragement of those who desire to do the same.

Each testimony is an actual occurrence I experienced personally. At times there were others present. I can only give account of the way I saw it. Often others may not remember it the same way or do not recall the event at all. I liken this to the four gospels. Each gospel was recorded in the manner in which they experienced and remember what Jesus both taught and did. So shall each of us be diligent to tell our good news the way we see and hear it. I must say, it was not only exciting to experience these phenomenal events, but it has been most rewarding and beneficial to learn the truths the Lord intended to teach me as He manifested His great power.

It is my prayer that you, too, will be encouraged as you have time to read these accounts. And keep in mind: we are all called to be partakers in His divine nature!

The Origin

I had just finished preaching at a church in Spindale, N.C. and was going to be flying out that afternoon. The Pastor informed me that there was a family going to the airport to pick up their father who was an airline pilot and asked if it would be okay if they gave me a ride. Of course, it only made sense to ride along with the family. As we were nearing our destination something seemed wrong. The road signs were indicating that we were getting very close to Charlotte N.C., which seemed right to the driver but not so right to me. The problem was that I was scheduled to depart from Greenville, S.C. and their father/husband was flying into Charlotte. Whoops! That was a problem! Spindale is evenly distanced between both Charlotte and Greenville and it was too late to turn around. Our assumptions had obviously gotten the best of us, but maybe it would all work out being the same airline flew out of each of the airports to the same hub airport. Surely they could get me there as easy as the other.

As I approached the ticket counter and explained my dilemma to the agent I was surprised to hear her response. "Sir, you must be at the proper origin for us to get you to your desired destination." Yes, my assumptions surely had gotten the best of me. Is it not often that same way in our Christian faith? We just simply assume we can get where we desire to go without starting at our proper origin. A lot of times it is taken for granted that people know what we are talking about without us ever defining or laying good groundwork for them. I do not want to assume everyone knows about, or for that matter, understands what *prophetic evangelism* is all about. It is very important to know where something comes from to understand where it is heading. The origin is as important as our destiny.

Everything in our Christian faith must be centrally founded on the word of God. Jesus came to fulfill all righteousness and all the laws and the prophets. So, it is from the example and ministry style of Jesus that we find our origin of prophetic evangelism. My first thoughts of prophetic evangelism came from seeing, through scripture, how Jesus ministered to people. Jesus only did what He saw or heard His Father doing or saying. John 5:19,30. This is, in the simplest form, the basis of a prophetic lifestyle. It is important to be mindful that we are not talking about being a Prophet or a call to the office of the Prophet. A person does not have to be a Prophet to be able to prophesy. We are referring to being prophetic, which is, seeing, hearing, doing, or saying what the Spirit of God is leading you to. Jesus did nothing in and of Himself but only what the Father gave Him to do. You see, He was tapping into His origin, connecting with the "One" who had sent Him to do His will. God was Jesus' source, so in turn, Jesus became the resource of Heaven here on earth. Jesus truly portrayed the Kingdom of God coming to the earth and the will of God being done here just as it is in Heaven.

God uses the prophetic connection through people, who have a seeing and hearing relationship with Him, to reach those who are unable to see and hear Him clearly.

So what is evangelism? It is the winning of a soul to a personal commitment to Christ or revival of a renewed commitment to Christ; The active calling of people to respond to the message of grace and to commit oneself to God in Jesus Christ. It is the spreading of the good news of salvation with eternal life through faith in Jesus Christ and His death on the cross for the remission of our sins, giving the promise of eternal life through the power of His resurrection from the grave.

It is important to emphasize that evangelism has the intent to win people to Christ and not just to the Church. Quite often in our present day evangelism we have reduced the goal to getting people to visit our respective churches. Evangelism without the prophetic edge can often result in merely propagating religion and the prophetic without evangelism falls into judging people. (See Jonah) Jesus' whole purpose was to get people to know God the way He knew God.

³ And this is eternal life, that they may know You, the only true God, and Jesus Christ whom You have sent. (**John 17:3 NKJV**)

²¹ that they all may be one, as You, Father, are in Me, and I in You; that they also may be one in Us, that the world may believe that You sent Me. ²² And the glory which You gave Me I have given them, that they may be one just as We are one: (**John 17:21,22**)

I am in no way implying that we should not want people to go to church. If someone gets to know God, like Jesus knows Him, as a Father and Friend, as Lord and Savoir, they will want to assemble with other believers.

Being prophetic is like issuing forth rivers of living water and evangelism is spreading the seeds of the word of God. Jesus told the woman at the well that He could give her living water and, if she drank it, that she would never thirst again. We know, through the prophet Ezekiel that everything lives where the river flows. As followers of Jesus we are to sow seeds like a farmer, let the living water flow and saturate them, and then expect a great harvest. The literal definition of a seed is, "the essential element that transmits life." The end result of prophetic evangelism is sowing and watering and trusting God to bring the increase.

It is very evident that Jesus ministered in a prophetic manner and I, for one, desire to follow in that pattern. For instance, when He was ministering to the woman at the well, as I mentioned earlier from John chapter four, the woman was ready to receive this living water that would cause her to never thirst again. Then, as if out of nowhere, Jesus told her, "Go call your husband." The woman replied that she did not have a husband and Jesus told her she answered well. He continued and revealed that she had already had five husbands and the man she was now living with was not even her husband.

Her reply…. "Sir, I perceive you are a prophet." We see here that as Jesus was sharing with her the gospel message of eternal life that He used prophetic knowledge to astound the woman. It caused her to go running into town and telling everyone, "Come see a man who told me all I ever did. Could this be the Christ?" Yes ma'am! This certainly is the Christ.. the Anointed One.. the Son of the Living God! As Christians, we not only take on the name of Christ but we also (are called to) take on the likeness of Christ as anointed sons of God. That is what the lost and dying world is waiting for…."the revealing of the sons of God," people who minister like Christ and who are like Christ.

Hey DeVries

Before I gave my life to Christ, I tried desperately to get myself free from addictions to drugs, alcohol, and immorality. In this quest for freedom, I went as far as enlisting in the United States Marine Corp in hopes of getting on a new path. As it is with any addict, the best way to quit is to use one more time. In the final days before my departure to boot camp, I indulged in the use of cocaine. Within the first twenty-four hours of basic training, I was given a drug test. I was hoping that all illegal chemicals would have been purged from my body, but they weren't.

Since I was excelling as a soldier and I was rated number one in my class, my drill instructor recognized my sincerity to better my life and to serve the country with vigor. He chose to see if there would be any way possible for me to be forgiven of my wrongdoings and remain in the U.S.M.C. After a long and strenuous journey of reporting to commanding officers, I was very relieved as each agreed to keep me as recruit. I was rejoicing and even started to go to chapel services when I first realized the jeopardy I had gotten myself into. This would be referred to as Jailhouse salvation... get right with God until He gets you out of trouble. It is the same as only being sorry because you were caught. I had enough knowledge of God that He could help me out when I was in trouble. I actually felt like I was right where I belonged—"boot camp." To me, boot camp was enjoyable. I was seeing a personal transformation taking place in just a few months. I am one who likes to see what has been done, and it was obvious that I was in better physical, mental, and emotional condition. I was getting ready to become a United States Marine, one who would live by the motto;

Semper Fi: Always Faithful!

The day I was being fitted for my dress blues, I was called to the quarterdeck and told to pack my bags. I had just completed the longest boot camp of all the basic military branches. I was days away from graduating, and had high hopes of making my family proud. I was denied the privilege of becoming a Marine due to my prior drug charge. This order came from the Brigadier General of Paris Island boot camp. I had never met the officer. All I was informed of outside of duty papers was that, "He did not want to take the chance on one of his recruits being a drug addict." In a moment of time everything I had worked for in the past three months was over.

As I was leaving our barracks, which housed forty or so recruits, I walked past the last guy on my way out, and he said, *"Hey, DeVries, maybe God is calling you into the ministry."* That had to be the last thing on my mind. God calling? In the ministry? What on earth was he thinking? Where did he get such an idea? I'll tell you what I was thinking about God? It was God that had just let me down! Ministry, yeah right! Now, how will I get my hands on some drugs and not have to face my family members? I was thinking anything but going into the ministry.

It was there, I believe, I had my first experience with prophetic evangelism. That young man spoke into my life what the Lord had all along purposed for me. I was being called into the ministry. It was a short but hard two years later that I gave my life to Jesus Christ. I had hit "rock bottom" and entered

Outreach Ministries of Alabama, which is a thirteen-month Christian discipleship program. Strangely enough, it had the nickname "boot camp for Jesus," being noted as one of the most regimented programs of its type. The founder and director, Jim Summers, would often laugh and say, "Greg, you just went to the wrong boot camp first." My mother still gets a good laugh at what I told her when she and my dad dropped me off at OMA, and I quote… "I may finish this program, but don't you dare think I am going into the ministry."

I believe that "last guy" was right. I was so distant from God that I could not get proper direction for life on my own. To get in His will for me I needed someone who could hear from God and communicate with me. One of those people was the young man suggesting God was calling me into the ministry. He turned out to be more right than I would have ever thought. Upon giving my life to Christ I felt the sudden urge to surrender my life to full-time ministry!

Let me ask you a question. How many times have you walked away from someone you wanted to minister to and said to yourself, "I felt like saying," "I wanted to say," or "I should have said," but you said only what made logical sense, or possibly nothing at all because it did not make sense to you? I often wonder, were those the very words of God echoing in your heart and wanting to get out to speak prophetically to that wandering soul? You desired to reach them evangelistically, hoping that your words would bring them life and not death so they, too, would not perish but have everlasting life. To offer someone everlasting life, we ought to be speaking words that have their origin in eternity. More often than not, the prophetic comes in the simple form of a thought. This is founded in Jeremiah 29:11, "For I know the thoughts I think about you." In one facet, the prophetic is God sharing His thoughts of others with us to share with them. As we speak prophetically we are not speaking only on His behalf, but also in His behalf. This enables the one we are speaking with to truly come to KNOW Him and not just to know about Him.

Instead of walking away saying "I should have said" or "I could have said"…let's leave them saying, "Only God could have known that", or "I perceive you as a prophet."

As you continue in the words of this book, remember it is merely a resource to help encourage you to become more prophetic in your evangelism. Resources produced by man are great; however, they are just a tool and written to spur you on to "dive" into the Word yourself. Let's not just rely on resources when we can tap into the Source Himself and become a resource. Even in our day, the world is yearning and longing for the revealing of the sons of God.

As the Word became flesh and dwelt among the people of His time while here on earth, so can the people of flesh become empowered in word and dwell amongst the souls of this age so they too can behold His glory.

The Son of God became a son of man so that the sons of men can become the sons of God.

Living the Dream

The prophet Joel spoke this prophecy and we hear it reiterated in Acts by the Apostle Peter on the day of Pentecost, "In the last days I will pour out my Spirit on all flesh, your sons and daughters will prophesy; your old men will dream dreams and your young men shall see visions." You may hear this passage of scripture several times throughout this book because of its importance to us all in the times we are living in. Being this is what God is going to give the Church in the last days, it must be for a specific and powerful purpose. Prophetic evangelism is closely related to the revelatory gifts and various operations, some of which are prophecy, word of wisdom, word of knowledge, discerning of spirits, dreams, visions and leadings of the Holy Spirit. We are even told to desire spiritual gifts and much more so to prophesy.

If you had a car but had no fuel, you would not be able to accomplish what you wanted or needed to accomplish with your vehicle. The same thing would be true if you didn't have oil in your engine. The engine would lock up and not be able to function. It would be essentially worthless to you and those around you. The church is the vehicle the Lord wants to use to bring the world, He so greatly loves, to Himself, but so often she (the church) sits around like a vehicle without any resources.

Our "resources" to the lost and dying world are the gifts and outpourings of the Holy Spirit in these last days!

Venturing out on a first mission trip with a few youth, a few adults, and a lot of passion and expectation turned out to be an adventure to remember. After a day and a half on our trip, I finally got the opportunity to call home and check on Gretchen and the children. You may be wondering why it took so long to make a call home. This trip took place in the 1900s; granted, it was the late 1900s—somewhere around 1994—but at that time, I, nor anyone else on our team had a cell phone!

After getting to a place where I could use a phone, Gretchen relayed to me that Spencer, our oldest child, who was three at the time, had a dream the night before concerning the team and myself. This was the first time he had ever mentioned having a dream of any magnitude. Spencer came to Gretchen early on the second morning I was gone and told her he had had a dream about Daddy the night before. The following is the dream as best we can recall:

The team and I had been ministering to some poor people on the streets but had not been giving out any food (which is exactly what had been taking place). While we were ministering, Spencer said that there were bad people trying to get us.

Gretchen asked if we were afraid or in danger. He said,

"No, they were okay because they had an angel with them, I saw angels on the van and in the van." The bad people then tried to come get him at our house where they (the family) were.

Gretchen then asked if he was scared. He again replied, "No." She asked him why, and He said,

"Because the angels that were here with us had water balloons."

You may be asking, "What on earth does that have to do with prophetic evangelism?" We affectionately knew one of our team members as Mama Mae. She was strong in intercession and often had prophetic insight. At the beginning of our trip, she had prayed, "Let there be angels in this van and at our homes, and let them be seen." Sometimes the prophetic in evangelism is not for those who are being evangelized, but for those who are doing the evangelism. The gifts of the Spirit are the fuel and the oil that keeps the vehicle going. In the great commission that Jesus gave His disciples, He instructed them to, **"Go,** and make disciples..." He also gave them power through the authority that was given to Him. That **"power"** is the provision of the Holy Spirit, and the *"GO"* is the instruction to the vehicle that carries His word.

Very often, people on trips have had dreams or a vision prior to going on the streets, and while on the streets, they experience exactly what they had dreamed or seen. Visions and dreams are part of our provision, as well, for "doing the work of an evangelist." It is another correlation between the prophetic life and an evangelistic heart. The result for God's Spirit being poured out on "all" people in all of these various ways is summed up in verse 32 of Joel 2.... "That whoever calls on the name of the Lord shall be saved."

Well Hello, NOLA!

The best I can remember, it all began by reading accounts of Jesus and how He ministered outside the temple—in the streets! It seemed to me that He took what was taught in the "temple courts," which would be, to us, like the Church, and did it in the streets. I found myself thinking, "Wow, maybe we can do this, too." But where, when, how? It was so intriguing; I had to give it a shot. I was a youth pastor at the time and had a group of sold-out teens and youth leaders who were feeling the same way, so we planned to take a road trip during Christmas break and preach the gospel to the lost. If you are going fishing, you might as well go where the fish are known to be, right? With that in mind, I thought, "Where else should we go but Sin City? New Orleans, LA would be our destination! Wow, I wasn't really ready to meet N.O.L.A., but it proved to be the right place and right time for us. I would have to say I was a bit out of my comfort zone.

It was the day after Christmas when we headed out to "take it to the streets." There were nine of us packed up in our church van ready for whatever God had in mind. About two hours into our trip, Mama Mae, we affectionately called her, stood up in the van and said, "Pull over!" You have to understand, it was no time to halt between two opinions. Mama Mae had an ear to the Lord and she had spoken! You just did what she said.. and so off the road I went and brought the van to a stop. She then said, "We need to pray!" This was when she prayed about the angels being seen, (previous story) but, she also felt we were to stop at the next rest area and do a prayer walk through it. We stopped, prayed, and got back on our way.

Now all that may seem senseless, but quite the contrary is true. It is simple acts of obedience that honor the Lord and assists in exercising our faith. If we will be faithful over the little things, God will make us stewards over much. I believe, no, I know, these small beginnings were essential to what happened the rest of the trip. Not all of the time when you hear the Lord's voice do you get the joy of seeing His manifest presence. It requires pure faith, which triumphs over fear and doubt.

As we continued with our travels, we came upon a stranded vehicle on the shoulder of the interstate. I felt compelled to help them. Now I must point out, they were on the other side of the interstate, headed in the opposite direction. I must also point out that the guys with me nor myself knew anything about fixing a vehicle. What could we do? In all actuality, it does not matter what we can do, only that we do what God leads us to do. It does not always make sense when there is a God calling. When I asked the two elderly gentlemen if we could be of any assistance, one of them replied, "Thank you Mother for sending us help." Thank you, Mother? I told him his mother had not sent me, but rather, I was sent to him by the word of the Lord. That did not faze him at all. He really had been praying to his Mother for help. We helped him the best we could. We even found the nearest Wal-Mart and bought the new tire they needed. One of our young girls had just received a gift card from Wal-Mart for a Christmas gift and was wondering why she felt she was supposed to bring it with her. While at that store, she knew she was being led to buy their tire, and she did! They were blessed as we parted, and one of the men said, "I am so thankful my Mother heard my prayers and sent you."

Keep in mind, you have to do what the Lord tells you to do in spite of what others may think or say. In the face of deception, we must remain faithful to the Truth. When you feel led to do something that, at the present, doesn't seem logical, consider it revelation and not calculation. The present, more often than not, is preparation for the future. How you handle the present will be preparation for the future.

Back on the road! It wasn't very long before we came upon a seemingly homeless man hitchhiking. It was not, and is still not, a normal practice for me to pick up folks hitchhiking, but I just knew this time it was the right thing to do. It wasn't simply that he needed a ride, but because I felt the prompting of the Holy Spirit. His name was Don. He was weather-beaten from many days, if not years of living a transient life on the interstates of America. His face was marked with scars, some, obviously left from some severe beatings. His face was soiled and he carried a very stoic expression. We had him seated in the middle seat directly in view of the rearview mirror. I could have eye contact with him, as well as, watch the road as I drove that van of precious cargo. Little did I know how precious that cargo really was. Through conversing with Don, I learned so much about the homeless and how to minister to them that would equip me for many years to come. He had knowledge, and a way of communicating his knowledge to us, that was beyond just one man's experience.

I was thinking about telling Don, "You are beautiful and fearfully and wonderfully made in the image of God." He would probably just have stared at me, thinking, *"Where did you come from? Can you not see the scars, dirt, abnormal features, or the pain of rejection and stains of failure in my life?"* But before I could say it to him, I heard the Lord speak to me: "If you really believe what you are about to say, then, kiss the son lest He become angry," immediately reflecting on Psalm 2:8: "Kiss the Son lest He become angry." I knew the Lord was instructing me to put my words into action. Okay, I did believe that Don was made in the image of God...so....God wanted me to kiss Don? My thoughts were probably just like yours are right now. "Now how am I going to do that?" Then it came to me. I had just been given a new, un-opened bottle of water. Actually, it was one of the first ones I had ever had (they were new to the market at that time). I asked Don if he wanted a drink of my water. I was really hoping he would politely decline. Fat chance! Without hesitation, he said yes. I opened the seal, handed it to him, and he took a drink. He was so filthy that I could see the water turn cloudy from the crust of dirt on his lips. Now it was my turn... this was to be the kiss. As soon as I put my lips on the mouth of the bottle, the anointing of God broke loose in our van! His presence was so real, actually amazing and astonishing. You have heard the scripture, "The earth is the Lord's and the fullness thereof." Well, let me tell you, that van was the Lord's and the fullness thereof!

Seated directly behind Don was one of our youth leaders, a young mother of two. The moment I took that drink, the Lord started a deep inner healing in her life. Now it is important to say, no one else knew what I was experiencing up to this point, nor did I know of anything the Lord may have been speaking to them either. I find quite often the anointing works best when we do not have it figured out. As a matter of fact, if you ever do figure out the anointing, it becomes religion. The young mother lunged forward and fell upon Don's neck and wept for what seemed like a good thirty minutes. I am not talking about some tears and little sniffles, but outright sobbing. All the while Don just sat there with no expression at all. The presence of the Lord was so great in the van, and a reverent hush came over everyone.

What had just happened? You have to know a little bit of this young mother's history. Both her father and husband had been heavily involved in the use and trafficking drugs.

Times got harsher and tenser as the years carried on for her and was left with many wounds from her upbringing. That day on our trip in the van she saw a striking resemblance of her father in Don's weather beaten, and darkly tanned neck. Once I took the drink of water, the anointing of the Holy Spirit started to break chains of bondage, unforgiveness and released the pain caused by the many wounds of her past. This incident went on for at least thirty minutes with moaning and groaning that could not be interpreted. All we knew was she had been set free, and Don never moved an inch!

There was a pastor in French Settlement that we were supposed to hook up with later that day and we were running late due to our "divine appointment." We finally made it to where we needed to change interstates to carry on to New Orleans. When we came upon the interchange, Don spoke up and said, "You can let me out right here." We pulled over, said a few good-byes, and out he went, heading toward the woods. There was chain-link fence separating the state property from the woods on the other side. I looked to see if we could pull into traffic and saw there was no opening. At that moment, one of our team members realized they wanted to give something to Don. As we looked out of the window he was nowhere to be seen. A bit stunned, we decided to call his name. Again and again we yelled for Don with no response! A holy hush came over us while we sat in silence. Right at the time I was about to say something, a black Ford pick-up pulled up to our side. I rolled the window down and the very enthusiastic driver of the truck asked, "Are you Greg DeVries?" I had never seen this man before, and I was a good hour away from where I was supposed to be meeting the pastor, whom I had never personally met. My response was simply, "Yes," that had a bit of "I think" tagged on it. He said, "Great, I am Terry, the pastor you are coming to do ministry with." He, too, was running late and had no way of communicating with us. He was praying for the Lord to help the situation and saw our church van on the side of the road. Needless to say, we were all a bit stunned at the very uncommon events we were experiencing.

Remember Mamma Mae's prayer? "Let there be Angels seen in this van...." Well, what we had seen in the van, we could no longer see outside of the van. Don was gone, but the essence of his presence with us lived on, and still does for me to this day. I have no shadow of doubt we were entertaining an angel unaware.

"Wolfman Jack"

It was late in the evening on our first night of the trip. We were getting ready to disperse to our respective hotel rooms when I asked everyone on the team a question. The question was, "What do you feel is your gifting?" They answered one by one, in no specific order, other than the level of confidence the few started in and the timidity the rest ended in. I still remember a few of their answers, but there was one, in particular, I will never forget, nor will I ever forget my response to her answer.

This certain young lady was the last to give her response to my question and what she said startled me. She was more apprehensive than any of the others answering, in fact, she seemed somewhat sheepish. She replied, "I have always felt like I had the gift of healing." It actually took everything she had inside her to say that out loud. Most of the other answers were not even listed among the nine spiritual gifts listed in 1 Corinthians 12. She had really stepped out on a limb. The Bible teaches us we can desire spiritual gifts, and especially to prophesy. So be it! Desire spiritual gifts! As if out of nowhere, I gave a response to her: "Well, tomorrow, you will get your chance to use it." From there, we headed to our hotel rooms to rest for the night. The thought kept coming to me as I moved toward my room, "Why did I say that?" and "Where did that come from?" I did not even know what tomorrow was going to bring. I had never been where we were going. I was a bit startled to say the least. I did not know then what I know now about the prophetic. Sometimes I think it is better that way. The less we know means the less we are involved and the less we can put our fingerprints on the works of God. We were getting ready to learn of His ways.

The following morning before we had breakfast, I taught a small lesson from John Chapter 4. My point was to reference where we find Jesus having to go through Samaria. The Samaritan woman was alarmed that Jesus, a Jew, was interacting with her. "For Jews have no dealings with Samaritans." My point to our team was that divine interruptions can lead to divine appointments or interventions. Sometimes you have to go in ways you normally would not go or be with people you normally would not be with. In others words, you will often times find yourself outside of your comfort zone. Before we went to eat, I told them, "Today we need to be looking for our divine interruption."

We ended up eating at The International House of Pancakes on Highway 90 in Biloxi, Mississippi on the coast. The restaurant was busy with hungry customers still enjoying the holiday season. We had just finished eating our meal and were waiting on our ticket. It was busy and it seemed to be taking awhile, so a few of our team members had stepped out to get some fresh air. One of them was Momma Mae. She shortly returned to inform me that a delivery truck blocked us in. I recognized this as our own divine interruption.

Right then, I noticed a homeless man who had entered the restaurant. He was going from table to table, asking the customers at each table a question. Each table replied in the same manner. They were uncomfortably and obviously saying, "No" to whatever he was asking. Immediately I heard the Lord say, "Whatever he asks you, just say yes." As soon as I heard the voice of the Lord, I started to ask myself the, "What if's?" You know, "What if he asks for all my money? What if he asks me to marry him?" Any crazy idea or logical thought to which the answer "yes" would be very illogical to ran through my head. It was here that I was seeing firsthand the contradiction between my flesh and my spirit man. It was not easy but I knew I had to go with the Spirit of "yes."

He finally made his way to our table. Without hesitation, yet not making eye contact, he said to me, "Hey, can you give me a ride?" That's it, a ride? That's all I had to say yes to? A ride… our thoughts are certainly not His thoughts. All those thoughts I had were nothing more than the fear of man or the carnality that leads to enmity with God. His ways are always higher than our ways. This man was so used to rejection that he began to walk away before I even had the chance to say my "yes" from God. When I got the affirmative response out of my mouth he turned around and said, "Did you say yes?" Oh wait! A delivery truck blocked us in. How could I say yes? In all actuality, I was not just saying yes to the homeless man, I was saying yes to the divine interruption of God. What seems impossible with man is possible with God. As soon as I said "Yes" our ticket came out and we were heading out the door with our soon-to-be passenger.

As we approached our van, the delivery truck was not as close as previously thought. We were free to go! We were only going to be traveling a few miles so I tried to start connection before we got in the van, "Hey, What's your name?" Quickly he said, "Wolfman, Wolfman Jack!" He had the hair and the beard and all, but it was nothing like the jet-black hair of the famous radio DJ Wolfman Jack, back in the day, whose voice was known to millions across the country. Trying not to offend our new friend, I asked him, "Where are you from, Wolfman?" His reply, "My momma." *Great! I am not just with an unemployed comedian, but a homeless comedian who needed a ride.*

Once in the van, I asked Wolfman how we could pray for him and what were his needs? He told us that he had not seen his family for over six years and that he had dry tear ducts and no medication to help lubricate his eyes. Along with that, he also told us that he was blind in his right eye. Now was her chance, so I called the young lady with the gift of healing to the front of the van.

She was seated in the very last row of our van and Wolfman was seated in the middle seat on the first bench seat. I was in the driver's seat where I could see it all happening in the rearview mirror. I saw it all happen!!

It can be difficult to move around in a passenger van. You usually get tangled in the seat belts, step over the wheel well, and then into the step area. Through it all she made her way to where Wolfman sat. He sat there motionless staring straight ahead. As the young lady laid her hand on the back of his head and began to pray, everyone else laid hands on him and commenced to pray as well. As in the book of Acts when they "all lifted their voices to pray," so it was that morning in our van.

What happened next was truly amazing. I could not actually tell what everyone was praying, but I could tell they were praying for the same reason. I looked up and noticed tears rolling down Wolfman's face, yet he kept the same countenance all along, almost as if to say, "If I move, it might break the wonder and peace I am experiencing right now." I would say that he was definitely astonished by what was taking place. His face said it all, "These people seem to care." And not only were they praying for his eye to be healed but they were praying for every area of his heart to be healed. Remember he said that his tear ducts were dry? That was the truth. *They __were__!* He now sat there with tears freely flowing down his face.

As the team continued to pray fervently for every area of Wolfman's life, I do not think they even noticed what was taking place. The best I can recall, they all had their eyes closed, all except Wolfman, and of course, me. Then, what I saw next was awesome. Wolfman put up his right index finger, as if to check if it was still there. He would shut one eye and look at his finger with the other. He did that, back and forth, alternating eyes open and shut for a few seconds. Then he shouted out over all the praying that was taking place, "I can see! I can see!" The Lord had healed his blind eye and opened his tear ducts. Their prayers had been answered, and our young friend was used in her gifting.

Wolfman's very next words were, "Take me to my friends." After his encounter with the presence of God having touched his life, he immediately wanted someone else to know, which is something I have seen many times since. He was now not only astonished but he was thoroughly amazed. I think the key behind it all was that the team did not merely pray for his eyes to be healed but for his heart as well. When you pray for a body part to be healed, it may very well happen, but the person may never turn nor change, however, if you pray for the heart, then there is the chance for everything to be changed because the heart is the wellspring of life.

Jambalaya Anyone?

Anyone who knows me very well knows I have a very sensitive stomach and I am a "plain-food" eater. Having roots in the Midwest makes me a meat and potato kind of guy. With that said, it should not be surprising that one of our first meals on the mission field was Jambalaya. Those of you who do not know what Jambalaya is, don't feel bad, I don't either! One thing is for sure. It is more than just meat and potatoes. I don't think anyone else on our team from Alabama knew what this Louisiana cuisine was either. It was a first for each of us.

Even though this was our first mission trip, we knew we were supposed to eat what was offered to us, and eat it we did. It got the best of us. Many of our team members literally got sick and none of us went back for seconds. Because this is a favorite dish in Cajun country, our hosts had proudly made a large amount. There was so much left it looked like we may be eating this for the duration of our stay. That is something I was sure we were not going to be able to do, but how would we ever get out of such a predicament?

Then the thought came to me. What if we used the leftovers to feed the homeless that night while we were on the streets of New Orleans? Everyone, including our hosts, thought that was a great idea. Only God can make a way when there seems to be no way! We ended up having seventy to-go plates filled with

Jambalaya and a few pieces of French bread. Now, we know that Jesus used five loaves and two fish to feed the multitude because that was what was on hand that day to bless and multiply. Fish and bread were two of the main staples for Jewish people in that day. So, here we are and all we had to offer was Jambalaya and French bread, which are some of the main staples to the folks of Louisiana.

I really do not know how to describe what took place that night in the French Quarter. We unloaded all the meals from our van and took them up on the Moonwalk, right next to the famous Café Dumonde. It was going to be one of our youth girl's responsibility to hand out the meals while the rest of us went out and invited the homeless to come and get a free meal. Within minutes, the word spread about the free plates of Jambalaya and the line formed, about twenty people deep, for at least thirty minutes.

After thirty minutes, the line kept a pretty steady flow for another half hour. Just as soon as the line would die out, there would be just one meal left. Then three more would come up for the plate, and once they were served, there was one plate left. This took place for well over two hours. Every time someone walked up, there was still a plate to be served. We did not have to turn away anyone! I know this is hard to believe. To be honest with you, it is still difficult for me to wrap my mind around it, but that is what faith is for—to believe outside of what your carnal mind can already comprehend. Faith is for miracles! A miracle is something that defies the laws of nature…something only the one who created nature can do!!! **Jambalaya anyone?**

Pure Religion

In our weakness, He is made strong. We had spent a few days with our host church before going to the Big City of New Orleans. We sorted clothes in the thrift store, cleaned a church, volunteered at a pregnancy crisis center, and had times of worship and prayer, along with some teaching. This mission trip was going great so far. It was late in the afternoon, after we had completed our task for the day. We were motoring down the road when Pastor Terry asked me, "What is pure religion?" Of course, I knew the answer according to Scripture: "*Pure and undefiled religion before God and the Father is this: to visit the orphans and widows in their trouble, and to keep oneself unspotted from the world.*" *(James 1:27)* Memorizing the Scripture and living it can be two totally different experiences. While memorizing the verse, you can build a picture of what it looks like if you were to act upon it. I have come to find it rarely ever works out the way we might think it to happen, verifying, once again, that His thoughts are not our thought and His ways are higher than our ways!

Upon my answer to Pastor Terry, he looked over his left shoulder and began to make a u-turn on the country highway on which we were traveling. Within minutes, we were pulling into the local nursing home. I have to tell you emphatically, that was not my thoughts of "visiting the orphans and the widows in their trouble," as a matter of fact, one of my biggest fears since being a child was visiting nursing homes. I would be hit with great anxiety and could barely handle the smell that is commonly associated with nursing homes. I now had to become the "fearless leader" as we were approaching the doors of my fears. All we had to go on was Pastor Terry telling us, "Go to every room and invite them all to meet with us in the dining hall."

After uttering a silent, but desperate, prayer for faith to triumph my fears, the doors were open. To my total amazement and sincere relief, there was a very pleasant fragrance that filled the halls. I was in a "wow" moment! I knew instantly that the Lord was up to something. I was filled with great expectancy now that my faith was experiencing victory over my fears. This newfound faith was also elevating me beyond my unbelief. I really believed that these precious souls had not only great value but purpose as well.

While we were in the dining hall, I was drawn to speak to a woman who was by herself and confined to a wheelchair. She was hunched over and looked to be well into her eighties. I stooped down to start small talk, not knowing if she would even be able to respond to me. I was elated to find that she could hold a conversation; however, I was surprised at her response, "You had better get away from me. He is going to get jealous." I thought, "This is going to be interesting. She thinks I am trying to flirt with her. She surely has lost her mind and is drifting." I told her not to worry, and no one will get jealous. "Oh, yes, he will; he is looking over here right now." Out of curiosity I had to ask. "Who is looking over here?" She said, "My husband, and he is mad at us!"

Sure enough, I looked in the direction she motioned toward and there was a man who, like her, looked well into his eighties and crouched over in his wheelchair. He was scowling at me, as if to say, "You better get away from here!" Through further conversation, I found out it really was her husband, and he really was mad at us for talking. Trust me, the farthest thing from my mind was coming to the nursing home to try to find a date. These two had me all wrong, but I could still sense that God was up to something bigger than what I could think up. Not only was he her husband, but I found out that he was abusive and they were not allowed to room together. As recently as the week before, he had been in her room and abused her by aggressively running into her with his wheelchair. She was really scared and meant it when she said I had better leave if I did not want to get hurt.

Keep in mind that I had just overcome my fears of nursing homes. Now I was with a woman who was battling her own fears, which stemmed from spousal abuse. She was very unforgiving, justifiably so, for the state she was in. This is something that she had lived in all her married life, which was not as long as you might think. As I said, they looked like they were well into their eighties. They were both in their mid-fifties! Each of them had an aging-degenerative disease. At that moment, the Lord revealed to me that she was being eaten away by fear and unforgiveness, and he was being debilitated by his jealousy and bitterness. I shared the love and forgiveness of Jesus, and she responded in prayer for forgiveness and healing and wanted to forgive her husband. She even believed that God could restore her marriage.

I went over and shared with him, as well, and he, too, responded to the gospel message, asking Christ for forgiveness and healing. Now he also was open to restoration. As I wheeled him over to meet with his wife, they both began to weep and hold hands. Both of their backs straightened up as well. You could see life coming into their weary bodies. It was equivalent to the fragrance that filled the nursing home taking away the stench that used to stabilize my fears. I asked them if they would like to renew their vows. Clenching their hands, they both agreed that is what they wanted to do.

Pastor Terry was at the piano by this time, playing various hymns and worship choruses. I asked him if He could play the wedding processional because we were about to have a wedding. He gladly obliged our request. Someone even found some fresh cut flowers. Everyone gathered around to witness this renewal. It was a sight to behold to see these two reunite in their wedding vows. When it came time to say, "You may kiss your bride," that is exactly what he did!

"This Guy Can't Move"

You know how one thing leads toward another? Well, it is like that with this story. One story leads to another, so this is a two-part story. The first part is something I have not told very many times, knowing that a lot of people may struggle with it, but I have prayed numerous times for the Lord to let me be truthful and not to fabricate or misrepresent anything regarding these testimonies. With that said, it is important to tell the truth, the whole truth, so help me God!

After being on the streets of New Orleans for a few days, I was amazed at the power of alcoholism that we were encountering. As I was praying about it, the Lord spoke to me. He instructed me to take our team out to a nice restaurant and to have a meal with them. Prior to the meal, we were to take communion together, but this was not supposed to be the way we always took communion in the church. I was urged by God to order a loaf of bread and a glass of wine. Yeah, I know. You think it is tough for your religious mind to be reading this… you should have felt what it was like hearing it in the spirit. He told me if we would take communion this way together, we would see the power of alcoholism broken. It was worth a try because nothing else was working.

I ordered the wine and bread and told the team what we were about to do. They all looked at me very intently. I gave each one of them the option to bow out without being judged or looked down upon. Some of the team had had problems with alcohol in the years before knowing Christ, and, like me, had not had any since their conversion. There were even some on our team who had never had a sip of alcohol before. This was a great challenge, and every one of us unanimously took that challenge as a mandate of the Lord. There was a very sobering spirit at the table with a real sense of expectancy, as well.

What happened next was one of the most powerful experiences I had ever had. After praying over the bread and partaking, I then prayed over the glass of wine and "took and drank." Upon taking that drink of wine, I knew I had just stepped into a victory I would have otherwise never known. I had no desire for more than the drink I just took, and I was totally satisfied with what I had just taken. I actually felt healing go into my body. I realized that what had, at one time, held me in addiction now had no hold on me at all. I had victory over alcohol. Sure, I had been "walking in victory" by not having a drink in so many years, but I had never been confronted by it since. I had merely gone without. But now I knew I controlled it and it did not control me. I had overcome.

Hallelujah!

The victory came in realizing I was not drinking wine, nor grape juice, if that may be the choice provision for one to partake in communion. I was by faith drinking the blood of the Lamb who was sacrificed for my sins and healing. This wine was representative of the blood of Jesus that breaks the power of sin and washes us whiter than snow. Our faith is our victory that overcomes the world (1 John 5:4). I now knew that I had victory. It brought me to a new place of authority. Until we have victory over something, we will never have authority in that something.

After dinner, we went back to the streets to minister to those whom the Lord led us. It had gotten late into the night, and was getting rather cold, when all of the sudden, one of our young guys came running up to me and said, "Pastor Greg, we need your help. This guy can't move." So I followed him to the guy, thinking all the way that he must be paralyzed. To my surprise, he was standing straight up, but, as I had been told, he was not moving at all.

There he stood, a grown man, well into his thirties, with a full beard and wearing a trench coat. He honestly could not move under his own power. He just stood there. I introduced myself and he responded by giving me his name as Coniece. He then proceeded to tell me his story. He had been homeless for nearly a year, and had not seen his family who only lived a short sixty miles from the city. His family consisted of loving parents and a fiancé who had recently given birth to their son—a child that Coniece did not feel he was able to provide for, and he became fearful of failure. He fled to the city and was now homeless and in great distress. His present condition created much shame and further prevented him from returning home.

Two of our guys had stopped Coniece to minister to him, and they really said some things that got his attention—so much so that he became frozen in his tracks or, spiritually paralyzed. Now they did not know what to do. I asked Coniece if he would like to return home like the prodigal son and start a new life in Jesus Christ. He said yes, but he could not move. I felt prompted of the Lord to kneel down and lay hands on his ankles and command the shackles to fall off so he could follow us to the van to give him a ride home. The moment I commanded the shackles to loosen, he was able to move.

We headed toward the van. I started to call for the team to follow quickly because I was concerned Coniece would change his mind. As we were walking through the parking lot, halfway to the van, Coniece unexpectedly came to a standstill right next to a fifty-five gallon drum garbage can. We all froze, not knowing what to say. He reached into his trench coat, pulled out a full bottle of vodka that still had an unbroken seal, and threw it into the trashcan. He then reached into another pocket and pulled out a tallboy can of Budweiser and threw it into the trash, as well. It was at that moment we witnessed the power of alcoholism being broken off this man.

It then quickened in me to go to the trash can, open the bottle and the can, and empty them out. Why? Because I did not want another homeless person addicted to alcohol to come trash diving, find those two full containers, and think the Lord had blessed them!

On the way to take Coniece home, we spent the whole time hearing his heart and praying over him. We were so enthralled in ministering to Coniece that I didn't even know where we were once we got him home. All I remember is that we were entering into a neighborhood that was culturally different than the one we came from. It was late at night when we arrived at his parents' home. Theirs was the only house on the street that still had lights on inside. When we walked in the house, we were greeted by his father, and I noticed his mother was on the phone. She was obviously speaking to his fiancé. I heard her say, "Yes, he's home. Yes, I knows it's the Lawd (Lord). How's come I knows its the Lawd? Cause it's white folks that brought him home. That's how I knows it's the Lawd!"

When we were leaving their house, I could see the burden come upon his father's eyes as if to say, "How am I going to take care of him?" The Lord reminded me of the Good Samaritan and how he gave the innkeeper provision to care for the wounded man leaving the innkeeper in hardship himself. (Luke 10:30-37)

I reached in my pocket and handed the father a significant sum of cash. Immediately without a word spoken, the burden was lifted as if his concerns were answered.

The Feast

It was in my daily Scripture reading when this verse jumped out and caught my attention. Instantly, I knew this was something I was supposed to do:

Carry neither moneybag, knapsack, nor sandals...

There was no question about it. I was to go to the streets to preach the gospel. I was not supposed to take any money with me (no money bag). I was not to carry any extra supplies (no knapsack), nor was I supposed to take a change of clothes (no sandals). It was as if the Lord was sending me out as He sent out the seventy recorded in Luke, the tenth chapter. I just knew it to be true.

After sharing this with a few trusted friends who had the same passion and desire to reach others for Christ, it was decided that we would start preparing for a three-day trip to the inner city of Birmingham, Alabama. The dates selected were in the middle of the summer, and we had two months to pray and prepare.

Fasting and prayer are very vital to the effectiveness of prophetic evangelism.

What precedes the ministry will develop the procedure and the results of your ministry. Even as it is written of John the Baptist, "...he went before the face of the Lord to prepare the way of the Lord." This signifies intercession before intervention. We also know that John the Baptist lived a fasted lifestyle, constantly denying his flesh and the comforts of the world by eating wild honey and locust and dressing neither for fashion or comfort as he was clothed in camel's hair. Jesus also taught that some things only come out by prayer and fasting. The biggest result of prayer and fasting is to be free from doubt and unbelief. Jesus was not upset that they could not cast out a demon in His name; rather, He upbraided them for their unbelief. We fasted and prayed prior to the trip to get any doubt or unbelief out of our lives.

There were only going to be eight of us on this trip. I wish we could have found seventy with such passion and willingness, but that was not going to be the case this time. The only other instruction we were given was that we would stay in hotel rooms no more than four to six hours a night. The rest of the time would be spent on the streets.

Prior to our departure, I had been introduced to an evangelist who lived in Birmingham and served on staff at a church in the downtown area. I made contact with him to let him know what we were going to do and when we would be coming. He offered his assistance in helping us to get to know the area. We planned to meet upon our arrival and take it to the streets together. Once we arrived, he led us a few blocks from the church to a busy intersection called Five Points, which is located in an area known as Southside, Birmingham. There were people everywhere, from all walks of life! This was going to be great. After our evangelist friend gave us a little tour to become aware of our surroundings for the next three days, he had to excuse himself for some other business matters.

There we were, in Southside, Birmingham, at Five Points, in front of the Methodist church, looking at a fountain dedicated to reincarnation. That's right... a fountain dedicated to reincarnation. In the center of the circular fountain was a goat dressed in man's clothing. In one hand, he had a shepherd's rod, while in the other; he was holding an open book to be the Book of Life. All around the goat were frogs on lily pads, looking toward the statue, listening to the teaching, or reading, of the goat. This was most definitely a hot bed for spirituality. Having been to many cities that have a "five points" intersection, I had learned that it is quite often a breeding ground for occultic and/or demonic activity. The reason is that those associated with such lifestyle tend to gravitate to the "five points" resembling the pentagram.

We arrived during late business hours, and the crowd was more business-oriented, going from one office to another. Some came to do shopping in the boutiques or meeting at restaurants to dine. There were occasionally homeless people who would pass through, and a few would sit on the steps of the church and rest. After six o'clock, the crowd turned more toward a nightlife atmosphere. There were many clubs in the area, and it got louder as the night went on with the people drinking and the bands starting to crank up. Still, the church steps and the fountain were a gathering place for many to just sit for a while. This made it a great place to meet and to interact with many people.

As the night went on, the crowd slimmed. The people around the fountain became harder and coarser. It was a combination of homeless men and women and groupies of sixteen to thirty-year-olds who were selling or buying drugs. It was now the meeting spot for solicitation of all types of activities. It was not like anywhere else we had ever ministered. We came to find out later that we were not like any others who had come to minister there before, because we did not leave after an hour of presentation. We stayed and we stayed.

By Friday night, we had spent nearly twenty-four hours right there in Five Points. We were even on first-name basis with some of the regulars who made the rounds at the fountain. Still, we had become somewhat discouraged. No one was receiving or accepting what we were sharing. Actually, we felt rejected. We later found out they had labeled us the "Crispy Critters" meaning all that Christians want to say is, "You critters are going to burn in Hell if you don't believe what we believe." They wanted nothing to do with Christianity as they had seen before. We needed to get some new direction as to how to approach these folks.

One of our team members suggested we go the highest part of the city to pray and worship, to tear down the Devil's kingdom. At the time, there was a well-known worship song that had this line in it:

"We're going up to the high places
We're going up to the high places
We're going up to the high places to tear the Devil's Kingdom down!
Let's Go Up!"

We went up the mountain singing all the way… "Let's Go Up!"

At the top of the mountain, we discovered a lookout area that afforded a great view of the city. There was a statue erected of a Greek god named Vulcan. There were plaques mounted with prophecies from Vulcan over the city. Many in the city, and many who had traveled through the city, idolized this Greek god. This statue had to go—somehow, some way. I prophesied that in the days to come, it would crack at its foundation and have to come down. I prophesied into the winds and left the rest up to God. We had found the stronghold over the city and knew we would experience a breakthrough.

Before leaving the mountain, one of the team members found a placard under some overgrown shrubs that recognized Brother Bryan, who was the first Christian missionary to come to Birmingham. We felt there was a connection to our not only finding the Vulcan statue which held a stronghold over the city, but also that we could identify with the mission of Brother Bryan. The Greek god was manicured and well kept, but the missionary was lost in the overgrowth around him.

"Down the mountain the river flows and brings refreshing where ever it goes." That is what we sang coming down the mountain, knowing that we would bring refreshing wherever we went and to whomever we would meet. Not knowing the streets well in Birmingham, we ended up behind the Five Points area and parked our van alongside a city park. It was late, and the park was not well lit. There was something about being there at that moment; a freedom, so to speak, and with that sense of freedom we began to worship. The freedom was so real that a few of our girls started to dance in their worship. It was obvious that something had broken. We were free now, and we could bring freedom, as well.

We discovered that we were only one block from the fountain. As we got to the fountain, it was strange that there were not many people there that night. The few who were there were much more open to us. That is where we found out what they had thought about us. Many, earlier, (while we were on the mountain) said they were happy we were gone, because we were starting to get to them. Gone we were for **a** moment, back we came for **the** moment.

The next morning we arose and headed back to Five Points. Still not very familiar with the streets, we ended up at the park we had found the night before. Now, because it was daytime, we could see much more than the night before. The ground was hard and cracked due to the drought we were experiencing, along with the intense heat of the summer months. There were three A-framed shelters with picnic tables under each of them. On one of them was a homeless man lying asleep on the table. Next to the shelters was an amphitheatre seating area.

There was a fountain in the middle of the park that was dry and dirty. It was most likely inoperable or not in use due to the drought. Then we saw it. The marker with a plaque on it read:
Brother Bryan Park

We were stoked because we were on the land dedicated to the first missionary. We knew there was purpose in us being there "for such a time as this."

As we walked toward the shelters, I kept feeling the sense of the prodigal son regarding the man on the table. As I sat down on a bench to do a teaching with my team, I started to turn to the story of the prodigal son. As I was turning there, the Lord spoke to me to go to another passage:

> **"But when you give a feast, invite the poor,**
> **the maimed, the lame, the blind."**
> **(Luke 14:13)**

I knew it. No, we knew it!

I could see the revelation on the team's face. We all knew it at the same time. We were going to give a feast and invite the poor, the maimed, the lame, and the blind. It was going to be for them, this day and in this park. We had the plans of the Lord. Everyone was excited. "Let's do it" was the attitude. The first question that came to mind was, "When should we do it?" I asked one of the ladies in the group, because she was a mother, "What time would you feed your children dinner if these were your children? Her answer was not common to our standards because she answered ten o'clock. My thoughts were, that seems a little late. Then she said, "No! 10:30 p.m.!"

That settled it. We would give the feast at 10:30 p.m. We would spend the day inviting the poor, the maimed, the lame, and the blind. We had fourteen hours to tell Birmingham the Lord was giving a feast at Brother Bryan Park. Come one, come all! The following verses tell of another story where many were invited to a supper: As the servants went to give out the invitation for the feast, they found that many who they invited were too busy to attend and made excuses. Some had bought land; some had to tend their oxen. They were just too busy to attend the invitation of the Lord. The Lord said to invite the poor, lame, and blind, but those who deny the invitation will by no means taste of His supper. We knew that there would be some who rejected our feast but nevertheless, God had something special for those who were going to show up.

Before we headed out to share the good news, it dawned on me... how were we going to provide a feast if we had no monies to purchase the food? We came with no money. One of our guys confessed he did not have the faith to come without money and he had brought a twenty-dollar bill. I appreciated the confession and honesty, but what was twenty dollars going to do for us regarding a feast for the poor in Birmingham?

Then it hit me that maybe our evangelist friend and his church could help us. I called him and told him everything the Lord was revealing to us, that he was leading us to live out the Scripture. He had given us a message to invite folks to a feast and I asked if there was any way the church could help. He told me he would see what he could do, and for the time being, I could go to the church and get some financial assistance for the meal.

Off we went to Five Points. Lo and behold, some of the first people we saw were a blind man, a crippled woman, and some homeless people! We knew God was up to something bigger than we were. Before we had left the park, Cara, one of the girls on our team asked if she could stay in the park and pray for God's presence to fall like rain. Knowing this sensitive, keen, young lady and her heart for the Lord, I knew this was the Lord's plan for her to stay and pray. She stayed behind to pray for rain of the Spirit.

After an hour or so in the Five Points area, I wanted to go back and check on Cara at the park. Coming into the park, I met a young couple and invited them to the feast that night. They were excited to be invited. We talked for a while, and I found out they were planning to marry as soon as they could get off the streets and get a place for themselves. Their names were Johnny and Secret. As I spoke with them, I could see Cara still on her knees in the hot-cracked lawn in front of the dried-up fountain of Brother Bryan Park. She had been there now for over two hours. Seeing an eighteen-year-old girl on her knees in a barren land, crying out for God to move, just does something to my heart. I can only imagine what it must do to His heart.

As Johnny and Secret were leaving, I noticed the homeless man on the table starting to wake up. Once he sat up, I felt the Lord leading me to introduce myself to him. I introduced myself, and he told me his name was Hack. At that very moment I could hear the old Negro spiritual song in my head: "Swing low, sweet Chariot, coming forth to carry me home." I knew the Holy Spirit wanted me to sing it to Hack. I might add, he was African American, and I am Caucasian. It would seem more logical for him to be singing it to me, not me to him. As I told him I felt led to sing a song to him, the words just came out of my mouth: "I believe your mother sings this every night as a prayer for the Lord to bring you home." I had no idea if he even had a mother, or a home to return to, for that matter. He just looked at me with no emotion until I started to sing. He wept and said, "How did you know my momma sings that every night as a prayer to the Lord to send His angels to carry me back home?"

I had no idea. We do not need to know the details but only He who instructs. What does it entail to be used by God? Willingness and obedience to His voice is what it entails to get Kingdom results. I truly believe the reason God has used men and women are because they are willing and have been obedient even through the things they have suffered. Jesus learned obedience through the things that He suffered, and was obedient unto death, even the death of the cross. Notice the three middle letters in obedience. They spell die. Our obedience to the Lord will always require us to die to ourselves. On any other occasion, I most likely would not sing a song to a person..... only if the Lord asked me.

Right then and there Hack gave his life to Jesus! As soon as we said, "Amen," we heard thunder, the skies opened up, and rain began to pour down. It was the first rain in over two months; the raindrops were huge. It was like a monsoon in Alabama. We looked out in the field where Cara was praying, and I noticed that although she was in the rain, she was bone dry. Not one drop of water was on her. I said, "Hack, look at her. She is bone dry."

He said, "Can't you see it? The Holy Spirit is all over her!" Here the newborn is, seeing what I could not discern; however, I knew it was a miracle and a sign and wonder of the goodness of our God. The rain eventually brought the whole team back to the park where I was sitting with Hack. It was obvious that Hack needed to go home to his mother, and the only Chariot there was available was our church van, so off went four of our team members to take Hack to his mother. The others would stay and work on the feast for the night. It was about one o'clock in the afternoon, so we had nine and a half hours for them to return while we prepared the feast.

At the church, they gave us a twelve-dollar homeless voucher to use at the grocery store for the feast. You want to talk about a humbling and discouraging experience? To use a homeless voucher was humbling, and to only have twelve-dollars was discouraging. We bought peanut butter, jelly, bread, a few snack cakes and a gallon of water. That was all we could afford. By the way, the guy with the twenty dollars was in the van, taking Hack home. What were we to do? All you can do is what is in your means to do and let God take care of the rest.

While making the PB&J sandwiches, I called the evangelist again to see if he had found any help. I told him about Hack and the miracle with rain. Even though it did not look too promising for the feast, we were still moving forward on the word of the Lord. Notice that no one was, at this time, giving a prophetic word. Being prophetic does not necessarily mean to give a prophecy, but to hear God, to see what God is doing, and to obey Him. Our evangelist friend had not yet made any calls but said he would be there that night with whomever he could round up.

The sun had set and it had been almost seven hours since the van left to take Hack home. It should have only been a three to four hour trip at most. I was starting to get a little agitated but not yet concerned. Where were they? What could be taking them so long? All we had was our twelve dollars of food. We had invited literally hundreds of people to attend the feast we were giving that night. It was amazing how many of them told us they would be there and that the timing was perfect. Why was 10:30 p.m. so perfect? They told us that is when they usually go dumpster diving for food; restaurants throw away their excess after they close at 10:00 p.m.! Remember how Laurie changed the time from ten to 10:30 p.m.?

It was now after 9:30 p.m. and the van was still not back. We had no cell phones because we had no knapsacks. All extras were left behind. There was no way of knowing where they were or what might have become of them. The thought crossed my mind, "Is his name Hack because he has hacked people?" I was concerned and a bit worried, when two guys approached me in the park. No one else had arrived. It was almost like they were sent ahead to see if this were really going to happen. We greeted each other and one of the guys asked me if I knew who was going to be there tonight. I told him I was not sure. He then stated that the Masters of the Covens would be there. I simply said, "We will have to call on heaven and see who sends fire." If you do not know who the "Masters of the Covens" are, they are the warlocks or witches in command of the covens. There were supposedly three in the area. They had heard about us "crazy Christians" and were coming to see if we were real. Now I know why I said what I said when I said it, but, at the time, I had no idea.

When the clock struck 10:30 p.m., it was like a weird horror movie—the scene where zombie-like people start coming out of nowhere, all walking in the same direction. Watching all these people coming out of the woodwork was a few of our team, the evangelist, and his one friend he brought. To be quite honest, I think they were coming to check us out too. They had every reason to doubt; all we had was twelve dollars worth of peanut butter and jelly, some snack cakes, and a gallon of water. And the van was still not back!

Then, I caught a glimmer of hope out of the corner of my eye. I could see a white passenger van turning the corner.... but it wasn't them! "What have I gotten us into? Are they okay? Is the van okay? Will I lose my job as a youth pastor? We now have over one hundred people showing up for a feast and all we have is.... you know. I had my back to the wall!"

At 10:40 p.m., our van came around the corner and parked behind the amphitheatre area. Out came the team, laughing, and smiles on everyone of their faces. They were all there except Hack. He had been delivered safely home with Mom! When I looked closer I saw they had steaming hot spaghetti, warm loaves of French bread, salad with dressing, desserts, and drinks. Enough, it seemed, for an army to eat. Where did it come from? We had that feast all right!!! It seems Hack lived near Cara's grandmother and they swung by and cooked up a feast at her house. What a blessing!!! Our guests loved it and had plenty of it. We were even giving away the PB&J as carry-out's! We fed well over one hundred people that night.

After everyone had eaten, some of our guests were saying goodbye, getting ready to leave, when the evangelist said, "Since they fed you, at least you might want to stay and listen to what they have to say." With that, they sat down to listen.

First to speak was David, who was only sixteen years old at the time. He preached the gospel for a good thirty minutes, and it was a great presentation. He came to a certain point of his address and then looked straight at me, like, "It's your turn to speak." I stood up and carried on from where he left off.

It was getting close to midnight and while I was preaching one of the guys rose up and came to stand in front of me. He asked me in a garbled voice, "Can you heal me?" Without a thought, my response was, "No, I cannot but I know who can heal you." It was obvious he had a dislocated jaw. His chin just sort of hung loose. I laid my hands on his jaw bones and said, "In Jesus' name, be healed!" I felt and heard his jaw snap back into place. We both stood there in amazement at what just happened. He was healed!

He went back to the seating area, joining the crowd, and I continued to preach. By now everyone was very attentive and they were hanging on every word. Then, right in the middle of my message, one guy from the crowd yelled out,

"Brother, how ought we to pray?"

For a moment I felt like I was in biblical times when Jesus was asked the same question from someone in the crowd He was teaching. I immediately started quoting the same words that Jesus answered. We know it as the Lord's Prayer. At the end of it, we are told that if we do not forgive others then our sins cannot be forgiven. As I told them these words, fifteen to twenty of them came forward, wanting to forgive people in their lives, and to give their lives to Christ. We now had a small church sitting together on my right side.

No one had left the crowd and I continued to preach. All of a sudden, the guy who had been healed jumped up and ran behind me. He stopped, looked at the crowd, and said, "Peace in the Kingdom and play in the Garden." Then off he ran into the darkness of the night. I turned and told them there were two gardens in the Bible. One was the Garden of Eden where Adam and Eve fell to temptation. The other was where Jesus committed himself as the sacrifice for our sins. "You choose this day in which garden you want to live your life."

As many as thirty of them stood up and came forward to give their lives to Christ!

It was now 1:30 a.m. and we were just finishing up the night. It was time for us to return home. While saying our goodbyes, the friend who came with the evangelist said he wanted to make an offering. All he had was a Dr. Pepper and a five-dollar bill. As soon as the money was placed in my hand, I heard the Lord say, "As freely as you receive, so freely shall you give." I knew I had to give it away. While I was saying goodbye to Johnny and Secret, I felt led to give the five dollars to Johnny. I was told to tell him he would never be able to out-give God and as He gives, so shall he receive. I put the money in his hand and he stared at me in awe.

Later, the evangelist opened up his heart and poured out his story to me. He apologized for not being there with us during our visit to his city. He had actually gotten a little frustrated with us during our time there. He explained that most people came, gave out food, and left, but not us. We kept hanging in there. He had actually prayed it would rain so we would leave. He was feeling convicted for not being on the streets with us. Then he heard that we were praying for rain, too, and had not gotten wet! I had told him that day the Scripture we were living out. And it was the same Scripture he was studying to preach at a church the next day. So he called church members to come and help, and they were all too busy except the one who came with him. It broke his heart that it was the church that was going to miss the supper. He repented and came to join us in the park.

Once we got in the van to leave, Laurie passed up to me a five-dollar bill. I asked her where she got it, and she told me Johnny had given it to her. I told her I had given it to him to bless him. A little puzzled, she asked me when I gave it to him. "At the end of the meeting," I told her. He had given it to her before it even started, saying he wanted to help in what God was doing.

Give, and it will be given to you.

So it goes with salvation. Freely we have received the gift of salvation, so freely should we give the unfailing love of God to others.

Signs and Wonders

Signs and wonders are to follow those who believe even if some of the signs and wonders of God are hard to believe. Keep in mind, it is not the signs and wonders we are called to believe in. Our belief is to be in the Lord our God who never changes and with Him nothing is impossible nor is there anything too difficult for Him. (Heb. 13:8-NKJV)

It was early in my walk with the Lord and I was, at that time, employed by the Coca-Cola Company as a relief driver on a delivery truck. My job was to fill in for the guys who were on vacation or absent from work for various reasons. I never really knew what each day would bring. To be honest with you, I did not look forward to going to work each morning. I desired… let me rephrase that…I passionately desired to be "full-time" in the ministry. I was, in all reality, looking for signs of God's call on my life and wondering when He was going take me out of the secular work force and put me into the "ministry."

There was a fellow believer at Coca-Cola who was head of the graphics department there. I was sent to help him one day and we found we had a common faith in the Lord. He and I wanted to grow in relationship with the Lord and enjoyed talking about God so he started to request that I assist him on a regular basis. I was able to encourage him in his walk and we would pray together too. We hit it off very well and were blessed to have such favor to work often with each other.

One day he came into the shop and was very disturbed. He told me he was very sorry for getting me into the situation I was now in. He relayed that there was going to be some layoffs at the plant and it looked like they were going to let me go. I was no longer doing the relief work and they really did not need me to help in the graphics department. I told him not to worry about me because I was headed into the "ministry" anyway and the Lord had great plans. Actually, I was excited at the coming transition but there was a slight problem. They did not let me go. They let him go and put me in charge of the graphics department!

I honestly did not have the first clue of how to run the department. I did not have any degree or knowledge of graphic design anywhere in my being! Furthermore, it was all computer-oriented, and I was absolutely illiterate when it came to computers. What was the Lord thinking? It was during this season that I began to understand that ministry is not limited to a full-time staff of a church, a traveling preacher, a Sunday school teacher, etc. Ministry, according to Phil Smith, my discipler, is "issuing forth the fragrance of Christ wherever you go."

Let me share with you something that happened while I was working in the graphics department at Coca-Cola. It was a Wednesday afternoon and we had church that night as usual. I liked getting home early to prepare to minister to the youth but, to my dismay, I received a call late in the afternoon requesting for a sign to be repaired. Of course it was on the far side of town. Not only was it far away but it was a strip club! I frustrated, but I was also challenged to have to go to such a place to do business. Why, Lord?

I called Gretchen, told her of my predicament for accountability and asked her to be praying for me. I was wondering,

"How will I make the contact with the manager to let them know the details of our repairs?" I was fretting all the way, wondering how I would walk through this untainted. When I got to the club, I went in the door and placed my right hand over my right eye, which was stage side, and went to the bar to inform the manager of our arrival to service their sign. I turned and placed my left hand on my left eye and proceeded out of the building. I saw nothing!

Outside, we had a truck that had a platform over the cab, which allowed us to pull directly up to the lighted sign and work on it. This caused us to be a good ten-feet elevated, and standing head high, you would be fifteen to sixteen feet high. I had a helper with me named Robert who did most of the work on the bulbs and inside of the signs. I was there to help when needed and to oversee the whole process.

Now I was standing fifteen feet above the ground in the middle of a parking lot of a strip club on the afternoon of a church night. I was wondering, "Lord, why am I here?" Just then, a car pulled into the parking lot. As I curiously observed, I noticed a bumper sticker on the back of the car. It read:

WNDA: 95.1 Music from the Heart

It was an advertisement for our local Christian radio station. I thought, "Now these two do not go together"—a Christian bumper sticker pulling into the parking lot of a strip club. Then I realized... this might be why I am here.

As the driver got out of the car, I called out to get his attention. He looked around until he realized I was up above, standing on the truck top. The conversation went like this:

"Excuse me sir." He looked around. "Excuse me sir. Up here." His reply was, "Oh, oh, yeah, what is it? I had no idea where you were."

I asked him, "Do you listen to WNDA?" He replied, "Yes." I said, "Are you a Christian?"

He replied "Yes." I said, "Should you be coming here?" Then he caught on. He was startled. He scrambled to get back into his car, all the time saying, "No, no, I should not be here." And off he went! Then Robert turned to me and said, "Okay, it is fixed." Off we went, as well.

Two days later, on Friday afternoon, I got another phone call from a disgruntled client. It was the manager from the strip club. He was angry that his sign was not working again and he wanted it fixed that day before the weekend. I was a bit agitated since it was late on Friday and time to be going home. But we had to return to the south end of town again.

I did the "right hand/left hand" routine again and I saw nothing!

While Robert was looking inside the sign to find the problem, a car pulled in. I looked down in utter amazement to see on the bumper a WNDA sticker. It was the same car with the same driver!

As he was getting out of his car, totally oblivious to my being there, I started to clear my throat and said, "Excuse me, sir." He once again looked around.

I said, "Up here." When he looked up, he scurried back to his car as fast as he possibly could, all the way saying, "I am not supposed to be here! I am leaving." Robert turned to me and said, "There is nothing wrong with this sign. It is working just fine, and off we went.

All the while I had been working on a sign and wondering what the Lord's plans were for my life. He was working a sign and wonder in another man's life to hopefully keep him from entering into bondage of the sin nature.

Being in the right place at the right time can bring about righteous results. It is not where you are, geographically, that makes you right with God, but where you are in your heart that can make things right wherever you are.

A Father's Kiss

I had just recently become full-time youth pastor for our church. It was a Tuesday afternoon, and I was sitting at my desk when the phone rang. I gave the proper greeting, stating the church name, my name, and the polite "How may I help you?" I am not sure I was expecting the request that was to follow.

The voice on the other end of the line asked if we had anyone at the church who would come to make visits at the Downtown Rescue Mission. The conversation went on for a few minutes, and he asked if I could come that day. He sounded very sincere and interested in knowing more about the Lord. I was intrigued. I cleared my already clear schedule, and headed toward the Mission.

When I got to the Mission, I checked in as a visitor and asked where I could find Patrick. "Here I am," came the response from one of the guys in the lobby. Patrick seemed very eager to have our visit. His female friend joined us, in whom he had confided much of his thoughts and feelings to. It did not take long to realize that Patrick just recently had a sincere conversion to Christ.

He told me how bad his life had become over the past few years. He named drug addiction, thievery, lies, immorality, and almost any sin you could think of. All this had resulted in his homelessness, financial and emotional stress. He was by no means near being the person he was created to be. Not only did he refer to all that he had become involved with, but he also made mention that he had just given his life to Christ and had abandoned that lifestyle. He had even quit smoking and had been delivered from all his cravings for the things he had been addicted to.

I was very impressed. This young man wanted to share his testimony with someone of the faith. I started to encourage Patrick and gave him a Scripture that would encourage him and confirm the Lord's doing. So I began to quote to him Revelation 4:12:

"They overcame him by the blood of the Lamb and by the word of their testimony and loved not their lives unto death."

Patrick said, "That's my problem. There is one thing I have not overcome yet." My thoughts were "what else could there be to overcome?" I mean, the list he gave was pretty heavy. Trust me in saying it was not the short list! I honestly could not think of anything else that he could have added that could have been harder to overcome than what he had already stated. I asked him what could he possibly still be struggling to overcome. "My desire sexually for other men," was his reply.

Now you have to keep in mind this was in the mid-'90s, and it was in the era of the outbreak of AIDS. It was nothing as common as it is today, nor was there the education we have today as to the origin of AIDS and how it is transmitted. There was a social fear of where it came from and how you might receive it.

To be quite honest with you, I was not ready for this dilemma. I did not know how to reply. First, Patrick wanted to know if he was unable to shake his unnatural affections for men, as he had everything else, did that mean it was okay with God? However, he did not feel right about it. He wanted to know, from me, who was a minister, how to be set free.

Not knowing what to say, I replied, "Let me pray about it and get back with you."

I went back to my youth pastor's office, stunned. Now what? "Lord, what am I supposed to do to help this young man?" This was all new to me. After much prayer, two things came to me.

First, I remembered something I had learned from a brother in the Lord some years earlier. I had been a delivery man for the local Coca-Cola Company. On one of my route stops, I met a man I knew from a church I had attended while I was going through Outreach Ministries of Alabama, which was the in-house Christian discipleship program for men with life controlling substance abuses.

He asked me to come into his office for a few minutes to talk. I was seated across from him on a sofa in his office. He asked me a very pointed question. "If I were to come over there and put my hand on your leg, what would you do?"

"I would jack your jaw. That's what I would do."

He said, "Do you think that is what Jesus would do?"

It was as if someone had just stuck a two-edged sword right into my heart. I was so convicted. Of course not! Jesus would have not reacted like I thought I should, or, for that matter, like I thought I would. No, He is not like us, but we are supposed to be like Him.

This was now coming back to me. You see, I was not ready to deal with a guy who had homosexual desires, and what was he doing calling me anyway? Here now was my chance to find the way Jesus would respond and not react. It was one of those "WWJD" moments. What would Jesus do?

The second thought that came to me was to invite Patrick to a special youth service I was speaking at that coming Sunday night. It was just two days away, and I thought he would enjoy coming with me and our youth group. It was a way of reaching out to befriend him. I also hoped something would happen that night that would allow him to experience freedom from his bondage.

I called him back and made the invitation. He accepted and was very excited. I made plans for us to stop by and pick him up on Sunday afternoon.

When we got there to pick him up, we were pleasantly surprised to find that he had unexpected visitors. His mother had come to see him, along with her friends who lived next door to her. They were happy to know about his recent changes and to find out he was on his way to church.

As we were getting ready to depart, I felt the Lord impress me to gather everyone in a circle and have a time of prayer. As we all started to circle and hold hands, I sensed the Lord prompting me to call Patrick to meet me in the middle of the circle. There were probably fifteen of us gathered. Gretchen, my wife, and our youth group were present.

As Patrick started to walk into the middle of the circle, again I sensed the Lord leading me to do something. He was telling me to give Patrick a kiss on the forehead. This was to be the kiss of masculine affection, of a father, which he had never received from his own dad. While I was approaching him, I was noticing the beads of sweat on his forehead right where I was supposed to give him a kiss. Now keep two things in mind: one, he was struggling with homosexual tendencies and had asked me how to get free from it; and I was getting ready to kiss him!

Secondly, I was one of those folks who did not know how AIDs was contracted. Could it be through sweat and saliva glands? We did know the higher rates of probability were active in the homosexual lifestyles, and this was really taking me out of my comfort zone.

All along, Gretchen was sensing the very same thing about me giving him a kiss on his forehead, and she was having the same thoughts about the sweat and what could possibly become of it. Our concern for Patrick outweighed my fear. I know sometimes there is a price for obedience, but God will protect us when we obey Him. I knew I heard God's voice and was going to obey Him.

When we met in the middle of the prayer circle, I spoke out loud the words that came to my mind.

"Patrick, the Lord has instructed me to kiss you on the forehead. This kiss will be the kiss you never received from your father as a sign of his love for you. It will be like the kiss of a daddy putting his little son to bed at night. This will be the touch of true masculine affection, which you have been seeking out." Then I simply leaned forward and gently kissed his forehead.

At that very moment, Patrick began to weep and break down. These were not just tears in his eyes that seemed to say, "That was touching or very sentimental or just a nice gesture." He began to sob and just melted to the floor in brokenness. He was broken free from the one thing he could not get away from. At that moment, he received the touch of God he so desperately needed. At that moment the Lord became the Father to this fatherless boy who had grown to be a man looking for the love of a man from what he lacked.

He was totally set free at that moment—so much so that he did not go with us that night. He left that day with his mother. He was free from all shame and guilt, and ready to live his life for the reason the Lord created him.

Was the power in the words I spoke or the acts of the deed I committed? I am not totally sure, but just keep this in mind. "Faith comes by hearing and hearing by the word of God." (Romans 10:17) and "faith without works is dead." We know that dead ministry will not result in a lively hope. Prophetic evangelism is all wrapped up in seeing and hearing what God is doing and saying. So we need to be both saying and doing!

You're a Christian,
Aren't You?

It was any other weekday in a normal week. We had errands to run, and one of them was to stop by the bus station to purchase a ticket for one of our teens who was in our youth group but had moved to Orlando, Florida. He wanted to join us on a mission trip we had planned while he was still attending church with us in Huntsville, Alabama. I thought our trip to the bus station would have been an "in-and-out" situation. As a matter of fact, this would be the first of many bus tickets I would buy. It's interesting to note that the first purchase was to get someone to join us on a mission trip. All the following tickets have been to send people home after they have been ministered to while in dire straits and in stranded cities where they did not belong. Gretchen and the children stayed in the van while I went inside to purchase the ticket. **"It should only take a minute. You guys can stay here; I will be right back."** That is what I thought at least. There are Scriptures that will help you be more fluent in prophetic evangelism. "For My thoughts are not your thoughts, says the Lord." And My ways are higher than your ways" (Isa. 55:8, 9). "Who knows the plans of the Lord but the Lord Himself." "And as for God His ways are perfect." (Ps. 18:30). We need to remain open to the Lord and His ways at all times or we may miss what He is doing or what He wants us to do.

Coming into the bus station, I headed straight toward the ticket counter. There were a few people in line before me. One was a lady I had observed coming into the station. She had been dropped off by a cab at the front door. The cabbie helped her get her three suitcases into the terminal, and from there she was on her own. Standing there in front of me, propped up on her cane, this elderly woman was waiting to purchase her ticket. I was wondering where she may be going. Will there be someone to pick her up? How will she be able to get her stuff out of the next terminal? Compassion for her entered my heart. I was genuinely concerned for her well being.

"Next," said the man on the other side of the counter, without even glancing up to see who he would be serving next. It was the lady with the cane. The woman stepped toward the counter as graciously as she could with her cane in hand and the suitcase sitting at her side, while telling the clerk where she intended to travel. Without any other words, the man stated her price and that the bus was out front and ready to load. She paid the fare and then asked if she could have some assistance in loading her bags. In a very unconcerned manner, the clerk replied, "We don't help people with their bags. You will have to do that on your own." On her own! It was obvious that was not going to be possible. She even told the clerk it was not possible in a distressed voice. She was trying to make a plea for some assistance, only to hear him say, "You don't have much time. The bus leaves in ten minutes. You'd better hurry."

I felt the Holy Spirit nudge me to offer my assistance for the elderly lady. I simply picked up her bags and said. "Ma'am, I will be glad to help you." Immediately the woman sounded relieved. However, the clerk scowled at me as I went to help the woman. Needless to say, he was not in the best of moods.

He seemed to have a very unsympathetic view toward his customers.

After getting her bags loaded, I headed back to the counter, only to find that my "next in line status" had now become "fourth in line." "This will only take a minute" idea was no longer a possibility. As the man in front of me would move forward, he would advance his bag, as well. Quite often, suitcases are referred to as "bags," but in all reality, they are well-manufactured cases designed to carry our clothes and other belongings, keeping them safe and protected from the wear-and-tear of travel. When I say this man was advancing his bag, I mean he was advancing his bag. It was a trash bag-one of the larger ones you would normally use for yard work. It was most likely one of those 55-gallon Hefty Lawn and Garden bag, and it was full!

Reaching the counter, he requested his ticket, and the clerk asked him if he had any bags. He said, "Yes," and pointed at his bag on the floor. To that, the clerk responded, "You can't take that on the bus. It has to be a suitcase."

Alarmed, the man said that it was all of his belongings, and he could not part with it. Unconcerned, the clerk told him he could not take it with him on the bus. Once again, being next in line, I was in a front-row seat to hear and see how this clerk was unsympathetic toward his customers. The Holy Spirit prompted me to say something. I leaned around the man and asked the clerk. "Where does it say on the ticket that your belongings cannot be in a bag and have to be in a suitcase?"

I know one may think it was none of my business, and they may be right, but prophetic evangelism is being about the Father's business! Jesus said He must work the works of Him who sent Him. We need to have the same mindset that Christ had and be about the Father's business. Remember when Mary and Joseph lost God? They traveled a good distance before they realized Jesus was not with them. Returning to where they had been, they found Jesus seated with the elders of the city. A child sitting amongst the elders would cause many to think that their conversations were none of His business. Jesus told Mary and Joseph. "You should have known I would be about My Father's business" (Luke 2:49).

The clerk looked at me as if to say, "When did this become any of your business?" Then he realized it was the same guy who had helped the elderly woman with her belongings. He seemed a little puzzled at my constant involvement, then he gruffly told the man to go ahead and take his bag on the bus. At that moment, I realized the man could not bend down to pick up his bag due to some type of physical limitation. I knew the Lord wanted me to help him load the bag, so I again stepped out of line and helped him get loaded.

Now for the third time that day and in that line, I was third or fourth, and I was a little concerned what Gretchen and the children were thinking while sitting in the van.

The person in front of me was a young African American girl, and she was pregnant. She was no more than sixteen years old. She was alone and seemed a little nervous waiting in line. I had noticed her when I first came into the station. She was seated quietly, all to herself, obviously waiting for her bus to arrive. When it came her turn at the counter, she asked the clerk when the bus to Florence was to depart. With no sentiment at all, he said that it had already left thirty minutes before. She was shocked and said, "You told me you would let me know when the bus was here and which one I should board." He gave her a pat answer that the announcement was made on the intercom. Somehow I could tell she was expecting a more personal announcement. This place was new to her, and she was nervous and had every right to be, but, again, he did not care. She then asked, "When will the next bus be leaving?"

"The next bus to Florence will not be here for another twenty-four hours." She was devastated. She turned with her head hung low and walked back to her seat, as if to say, "I am doomed." Can you imagine being sixteen years old and stranded at the bus station for twenty-four hours; not to mention being pregnant?

I stepped to the counter and he looked at me as if to say, "Well what are you going to do now?" I simply requested my ticket and made the purchase.

I went to the van and asked Gretchen if it would be alright if we gave a young girl a ride to Florence, which is seventy miles west of where we were. She readily agreed, and I went to see if the girl would like a ride. I approached her carefully, told her my family was in the van, and we were willing and able to transport her to Florence right then.

To my surprise, she immediately accepted my offer without thinking twice. She seemed very comfortable with the whole idea. It was as if the worry and concern had lifted off of her in a moment's time, and off we went to the van.

I let her in the side door and then loaded her luggage in the rear. I hopped in the front seat and started the van. Right then she said to me, **"You're a Christian, aren't you?"**

I replied, "Yes I am, are you?" She said, "No, I am not, but my grandmother is." "Why aren't you?" I asked her. "I am not ready," she said. I told her, "We will never be ready to become a Christian, we become a Christian so we are ready for when Christ returns." The whole way to Florence we shared the love of Christ with her and prayed with her, hoping that she too would give her life to the Lord. I wish I could say she accepted Christ as Savior that day, but that is not the way it turned out. As it is in all types of evangelism, it is the same with being prophetic in your evangelism. Some water, some plant, but God gives the increase. Sometimes we are watering, sometimes we are planting, and other times we will be harvesting.

She made an interesting statement at the beginning of our trip that I want to share with you. I had asked her how she knew I was a Christian. And this is what she said to me:

"I watched you in the bus station at the way you helped those people. When you turned on your van, the stereo was on a Christian station."

Wow! And I thought I was the one who noticed her!

What if I had not been kind and compassionate in the station? Would I have ever gotten the chance to meet her? Would she have gotten in the van? We are all called to be servants and not overlook the needs of people.

What if it had been playing some of that music that talks about loving another man's wife and bar doors swinging? How about some hard-core rap that speaks of, "You bleep, bleep, kill you cops" kind of music or maybe some oldies but goldies? She would have most likely seen me as another "good ole boy, her homie, or maybe just a nice man." But she saw someone who is Christ-like.

This is what I would refer to as lifestyle evangelism. Our lives must line up with what we are preaching, or it will fall upon deaf ears and have no authority. Maybe you have heard the old saying, "practice what you preach." That is usually said to someone who is living a different lifestyle than what he is preaching to others. Look at it this way—only preach what you practice. Make sure you have a lifestyle that will promote and support your prophetic evangelism.

I might add, if you are ever in a big city and cannot find a good spot to minister, find the bus station because it is always a great place to find a crowd that needs ministry.

You Will Never Guess

There I was again, wrestling with God, wanting to know if I was called to prophetic evangelism. Actually I was wondering if I was prophetic at all, or even if I was an evangelist. At the time I was pastoring a church in Huntsville, Alabama. It was a young fellowship with a lot of people who loved the Lord and were willing to share His love with others. I still enjoyed traveling and ministering, but I also knew I was supposed to be where I was discipling these young Christians.

It was in my early morning time of devotions that I asked the Lord what exactly was I called to do—pastor or evangelize? Immediately the Lord took me to a passage in the book of Isaiah found in chapter 49 and verses 1-7. I had been given this Scripture as a word of encouragement some years earlier by both the Lord and a person who was praying for me. It was verse six that leapt out at me this morning.

> *6 Indeed He says,*
> *'It is too small a thing that You should be My Servant*
> *To raise up the tribes of Jacob,*
> *And to restore the preserved ones of Israel;*
> *I will also give You as a light to the Gentiles,*
> *That You should be My salvation to the ends of the earth.'"*

It was too small a thing to **just** raise up the tribes of Jacob although that has always and still is a mandate on our lives.

Gretchen and I actually had a discipleship team at that time we called "The Tribe." The tribes of Jacob make reference to the people of God or the house of Israel, which meant to me, the church and the Christians that I was pastoring. There definitely seemed to be an implied message that I could carry more of a burden and that it was too light a thing to just disciple Christians. It was the next line that lit my fire. "I will give you as a light to the **Gentiles**... to the ends of the earth." I knew this was a prophecy regarding Jesus Himself, but I also knew that He was speaking to me and that He wanted me to be one with the Father just as He is one with Him. I realized he was telling me I can be and can do both, that is, to pastor/disciple the church body and to evangelize the world by giving them the Light of the World.

I came out of my time alone with the Lord ready to face the day, and yet wondering, "Was that the Lord, or was that just me?" Just a few minutes earlier I knew He was talking to me!

It was a family day, and we had family things to do. We needed to drop my son's guitar off to get repaired and numerous other errands to run while in town. After dropping off the guitar, Gretchen informed me she needed a potty break at the next convenience store. This was not out of the ordinary, because she was pregnant and needed a break frequently. Into the parking lot of the gas station I pulled. Not needing any fuel, I pulled right up to the curb leading to the door and there stood a man who was obviously homeless.

I thought this to be an opportunity to share the love of Christ with this man. I was only four feet away and the only thing keeping me from him was my van door. Out I popped and cheerfully spoke to him, saying, "Hi! My name is Greg. What's yours?" His reply: "I am not going to tell you."

I tried to pry it out of him, but to no avail. Then he said, "It is in the Bible." That got me guessing his name. "Is it John?...."

Is it Luke?.... Moses?... Elijah? After a while, I was running out of names and wishing Gretchen would hurry out of the bathroom. Then he said, "You will never guess it, but if you buy me a Baby Ruth candy bar I will tell you." No problem. I was going to be glad to buy the Baby Ruth to find out what this name from the Bible was, and how it could be that I could not guess it. While I was going in the door, he yelled, "Make sure it is a king size one!" And, "Oh yeah, get me a Pepsi, too!" It just seemed like he knew he had me... hook, line, and sinker. I just had to know, no matter what it cost.

I came out and gave him the goodies. He went straight to the Baby Ruth as if he had not eaten in days. He was really going after it and was thoroughly enjoying it. I was delighted to watch him and to see the pleasure in his face. Then it hit me, he has to tell me his name. I asked him, "So tell me, what's your name?" *You will never guess. It is in the Bible.*

Enough was enough. The guy obviously knew something I didn't. "I will never guess, and it is in the Bible." Once more a bit more sternly I asked him. "What's your name?"

"Gentile"

And he turned and walked away....

Now I was blown away. I was called to be a light to the Gentiles. That is exactly what the Lord had spoken to me that very morning. Was that an angel I just encountered? "Lord is that You?" I was utterly astounded and surely amazed.

He was right. I would never guess and get it right. I really learned something from this encounter. We are not to guess at our calling but to know it by hearing the Lord's voice. Just as we are never to guess at what we are to say to those we are ministering to, we are to listen to the Lord's voice and speak only what we are hearing Him say and do only what we are seeing Him do. That is being prophetic in our evangelism.

He was also so right in saying, "It is in the Bible." Our calling from God will always line up with what is in His word. I truly believe that everyone who believes can find themselves in the Scriptures if they will just be faithful to get the Scriptures in them.

What Happens in Vegas Doesn't Have to Stay in Vegas

The previous week was spent in Denver, Colorado, at the YWAM base founded by our dear friends, Peter and Linda Warren. It was there that I was teaching a week course on Prophetic Evangelism. The class consisted of approximately twenty-five students and eight staff members. They were from ten or so different nations. YWAM (Youth with a Mission) is an international missions base in which people from all around the world are trained to do evangelistic world missions. What an honor it was for me to be teaching such hungry and serious Christians who wanted to share their faith with others around the world! Their motto is "to know God and to make Him known." I love it!

I flew home only for a few days before I was to meet up, in Las Vegas, with the team I had just taught at YWAM Denver. This time I not only got to teach the team, I got to do evangelism with them! I love the opening of the book of Luke: "These are both the things Jesus began to teach and do." This would be many of the team's first time out on the streets doing raw evangelism. For all of them, the concept of prophetic evangelism was totally new. This was going to be fun.

This would be my second time on the streets in Las Vegas. I am sure you are familiar with the industry in Vegas; it is a city primarily built on gambling. It runs all day and all night, nonstop. Tens of thousands of people are in that city trying their luck to strike it rich. It may seem beautiful to the natural eye to see the neon lights and the incredible architectural designs, but to the spiritual eye, there is no hiding the blatant love of money, which is the root of all evil. Of all the cities I have visited over the years, none has had such a spiritual darkness over them as Las Vegas. It is totally oppressive. I had asked a dear friend of Gretchen and mine to accompany me for the extra support of prayer and intercession. Well, that was not the only reason; she is great on the streets, moving strongly in prophetic evangelism, and she loves it. Her name is Cara, and I was grateful to have her with us.

I think it was on the second night that we went out to minister. We had spent some time in prayer and a little time in teaching. I always encourage the teams to be sensitive as to who the Lord is leading them to minister to, not to just pick someone out but to really feel led to the one He has for you. That was my emphasis that certain night: "God has someone for you to speak to, and He will lead you there if you let Him."

The older part of Vegas is much more conducive to street ministry. There is a strip about three city blocks long where thousands of people are continuously walking under a canopy of lights. As we entered at one end, I immediately noticed a young man sitting on a street bench. He looked as if he may have been homeless, but not as if he had been that way for very long. I could tell my heart was being drawn toward him with compassion, but I knew the Lord was telling me to keep walking. I must admit, I really wanted to go over and meet this guy! It was not for now. I had to keep going.

I walked from one end of the strip to the other and never once felt led to minister to anyone else. I was heading back in the opposite direction. Again, I went the whole distance and did not feel any prompting to stop and strike up a conversation with anyone. Then there he was, the guy I had first seen when we entered on Fremont. He was sitting on the same bench. Now I knew the Lord was leading me to go over to him. Without hesitation, I went straight to the bench where he was sitting. "Hi, my name is Greg. What is your name?"

He answered, "Jerry." I asked him where He was from and how long had he been in Vegas. He told me he had been there for a few months. He came out to deliver furniture from North Carolina, which was where he was from, just outside of High Point. He was in the furniture business and had gotten the opportunity to make a delivery to Vegas. Once he got there, he did not want to leave. When he lost all his money, ended up drunk, living on the streets, and homeless, then he wanted to go home but was stuck there. It was obvious he had been drinking that evening, as well.

He was hungry, lonely, and concerned. His biggest concern was that his mother and family would know that he was alright. But, because he was ashamed, he could not bring himself to make a call home. He was also concerned that the Lord had forsaken him and no longer cared for him. I asked, "Can I pray for you?"

"I knew you were going to ask me that!" He did not want to pray with me because he was embarrassed that he had been drinking and did not want to disrespect God. I found out also that his dad had been a pastor before he died.

I really knew the Lord wanted me to pray with him, so I just started to pray for him without bowing my head, folding my hands, or closing my eyes. He looked at me with a little smirk and said, "I knew you were going to do that."

This is simply what I prayed for him: "Lord, let Jerry know that you know where he is right now, and that you care for him. Let his family know that he is here and that he is okay. Make a way for him to get home…." Right then Jerry said, "Holy ____! I can't believe it! What are you doing here?"

From behind me, a man showed up and gave Jerry a big bear hug. He started saying how amazed he was to see him there and that his (Jerry's) mom sure was going to be happy to know he was okay. He went on about how Jerry needed to come with him back to North Carolina. It was Jerry's sister's boyfriend from his hometown!

Right there God showed Jerry an answer to prayer. He was blown away! Now stop and realize. What if I had stopped earlier? We may not have ever seen the sister's boyfriend. Timing is so important to what we see the Lord doing and to do what we hear the Lord saying. God is perfect in all of His ways (Ps. 18:30).

Jerry now had a way home from Vegas, and renewed faith in the fact the Lord loved him and had not forsaken him. God knew right where he was!

Sir, You Don't Understand?

One day, while in a casual conversation, someone mentioned the MSNBC news report regarding runaway teenagers in Portland, Oregon. That caught my attention, and I listened very closely. They told of how the news reporters would somehow tag the teens so they could track where they were meeting. To the best of my knowledge, it was not like tagging a wild animal (nevertheless, I wondered if these people were just working on a good and unique story). I thought, "If you are going to go through that much labor and expense, do something that is going to help these teens."

I did not have to think twice. I was going to Portland to meet these teens and see how I could share Jesus with them.

It was only a few months later that I got a phone call from a youth ministry that I had previously worked for, helping to cast the vision for the youth conventions they hosted around the country. They wanted to know if I would be able to assist them in doing one more event. I was interested, and asked the dates and the location. Of all places, it was Portland, Oregon! I told the host ministry of my heart for finding the runaway teens in Portland. They were very gracious and accommodating—so much so that they covered not only my flight to and from Portland, but they also covered my hotel expenses for three extra nights, allowing me to take some time to stroll the streets of downtown Portland.

After I went the first time by myself I could not conceal the passion that was now burning in my heart once I encountered more than 2,000 runaway teens living on the streets of Portland. I was going back and taking with me whosoever heard the call to go! Each year following, there were a growing number of folks who would accompany me.

I clearly remember one of my fondest encounters in Portland. It was the fourth year we had been attending and we had the largest group to date. I accompanied two of the girls with our ministry who were going to be doing the grocery shopping for the week. Cara and Heather had been with us in the ministry for quite a while, and they pretty much knew what we needed, so I was just "along for the ride." The shopping was taking longer than I expected, and I had already seen everything that interested me in the Safeway grocery store, so I just strolled around while the girls finished shopping.

As they approached the checkout line with two overloaded buggies, I followed behind them because I was going to be paying the bill. It did not take long to see a need to minister. Our cashier was not only checking us out, he was also carrying on a conversation with another cashier, and every so often he would talk to himself. It seemed as if every other sentence he would speak he would use the Lord's name in vain. It was not just a few times. It was non-stop, and my spirit was grieved. Here is something to be considered; if what grieves the Spirit of God does not grieve us, what's lacking? Could it be the absence or disconnect of our relationship or sensitivity to the Spirit of God? We need to be spirit-led in prophetic evangelism. So I prayed for the Lord to open a door for me to be able to minister to him. As the groceries were dwindling in our carts, I sensed nothing but the grieving in my spirit and an increased desire to speak into his life. Just as he was scanning the last of our items, he said, "Will that be all?"

As quickly as he asked the question, I turned and looked behind me in line. There was a girl in her mid-twenties who was holding maybe four or five items. It was not enough to require a buggy, or for that matter, a basket. She was very thin, almost emaciated. You could tell it was not her normal weight. She had obviously lost a lot of weight due to something unhealthy. Her eyes were sunken and glassy. There were many scabs on her body, especially on her arms. Her hair was very short and dirty. It was obvious to me that she was not happy with the life-style she was living. To be honest, she looked terrible, almost lifeless. My heart was now pounding, and I was stuck between ministering to her and the cashier who obviously did not know the Lord.

As I was turned toward the young girl behind me, I heard the cashier asking me if that was all. In the same moment, I heard the Lord say to me, "Buy her groceries." The first thought that came to me was, "But, Lord, she is a drug addict lesbian." Mind you, I released that thought quickly. That is what hap-pens more often than not—the carnal mind tries to interrupt the spiritual communication with God. As always, the spirit and the flesh are contradictory to one another. I wonder how many times we are speaking to someone, and we feel like say-ing something or doing something that makes no sense at all. It is contrary to our understanding, so we don't say it or do it. Then we walk away thinking, "I should have said it," and later we realize it was the Spirit of God prompting us. It is important to realize the conflict between the spirit and the flesh so we can overcome the weakness of the flesh and fulfill the desires of the spirit. This is key in prophetic evangelism.

I then turned to the cashier and said, "No, we are going to buy her groceries, too." He looked at me, a bit shocked, and said, "Are you sure?" Good question, I might add. We need to be certain of the voice of the Lord to be effective in prophetic evangelism. "Yes, I am sure."

As I turned to look at the young girl, she looked at me as if I were some kind of alien. Totally surprised, she began to speak to me as if she had just woken up.

"Sir, sir… Sir, you don't understand Sir, you do not understand. This has been… this has been…." For some reason, she could not finish what she was trying to say to me. She was totally taken aback, and it was a good thing she had already laid the items on the belt. Otherwise, I think she would have not let me have them. The cashier was already running them through the line. (I might add this was way before "pay it forward.") God is creative in all His ways. We need not look to the ways of others to find His ways- His are higher.

Once the cashier finished ringing the items up and giving me the total, he looked up and me and said, "God Bless you, sir." A far cry from using the Lord's name in vain!

The girl's part of the bill was fourteen dollars and some odd cents, or was it fourteen dollars and some odd *sense.*

She was shocked. As we moved out of the line, we introduced ourselves to her. She was elated to find out we were Christians and that it was the Lord who had us buy her groceries. She told us that her mother had raised her in an occultic religion, but she always knew that Jesus was real and had wanted to meet Him. She also told us she had been living a lesbian lifestyle, which she knew was wrong but did not know how to get out of it. The scars on her arms were from needles she had been using to intravenously shoot drugs in her arms. The weight loss was a direct result of her drug addiction.

She had just that day prayed in desperation that the Lord would become real to her and help her out of her despair. She was trying to tell me, "Sir, you do not understand. This has been the worst day of my life." But she could not finish the "… the worst day of my life," because it just became **the best day of her life!**

She not only experienced Jesus, she accepted Him as her Lord and Savior! She just met the Jesus she had always known existed. She had a profound encounter with the grace of God in her life.

She was in awe of the kindness of God, which leads a man to repentance, and she now had the courage to break off the relationship she was having with another woman. She knew she was not just saved but healed, and all the deception she had grown up around was now exposed and proven false.

After we prayed and chatted a while, encouraging her in her new found faith, it was time for us to go. We loaded our groceries in the vehicle and started to leave. While we were pulling out of the parking lot, I looked back to see our new sister in the Lord, still standing in utter amazement at what had just taken place in her life. His grace never ceases to amaze!

So, the next time you go shopping, it might become the best day of someone's life—all for the great value of fourteen dollars and some "sense!"

Can You Hear Me Now?

The Uprising event at our home church had just finished up and it was late. Our plans were to leave that night after the Uprising and drive at least to Montgomery and stay in a hotel room. The next morning, we (meaning the whole family) would get up and make it to Columbus, Georgia, to be with our dear friends Chris and Jamie Mitchell. We would be there for the weekend ministering at their Adopt-a-Block outreach and holding services at the church they were pastoring. We would not return home until the middle of the following week.

About an hour down the interstate I realized I did not have a cell phone charger for my phone. I didn't have a car charger or a wall charger and there was less than half a battery charge left on my phone. What was I going to do? If we turned back it would kill two to three hours of time and there would be no way to make our appointed time the next morning and be worth anything at all.

In the midst of wondering what I should do, I heard the Lord say, "Do not worry about the charger and do not buy one until I tell you to." That was peaceful at least for a few minutes, and then the old mind started turning every which way. What if someone tries to reach me to have me come and preach? Is the Lord going to keep me from having a phone for a long period of time? What if?, what if?, what if?... On the other hand, I had the comforting thought that I would not be hassled by any unwanted phone calls, but I may need to make a call myself.

We got to Columbus on time and were well rested. The outreach was great, and many lives were touched in unique ways. The services on Saturday night and Sunday morning were powerful and very effective, as well. Sunday, after service, we went to a Mexican restaurant with the staff from the church. After lunch we were returning to our hotel, traveling on a road I had never traveled before. I looked over and saw a Verizon sign for a store in the plaza that was to our left side. Seeing the sign, I knew in my spirit it was a sign from the Lord and time to get a phone charger.

I zipped into the parking lot and went into the store. The immediate sense I got when I walked in the store was that it was a very uncommon atmosphere. Every time I experience an uncommon atmosphere, I start to look for what is common to me to connect to, and vice versa. If I enter into an atmosphere that is common to me, like a church service, I tend to look for what is uncommon. And more often than not, that's where the Lord will have me working. It is associated with the spirit and the flesh being contrary to each other.

What was so uncommon in this situation at the Verizon store was that I was the only customer in the store. It was very unusual to be in a cell phone store and it not be busy. Usually you have to take a number or sign in your name for the next available employee to help you, but not this day. I was the only customer. I instantly had the sense that the Lord's plan was coming together; my not having a charger, and God saying, "Do not get one until I tell you to."

While I pondered my "lone customer" status I asked God, "Lord, is there some other reason you have me here right now?" Right then I heard one of the two girls who were working in the store speak so loudly that I thought I was supposed to be in their conversation. She was telling her co-worker what she had dreamt the night before. She could not figure out what it all meant. She said she was even going through a dream interpretation book, yet she still could not make ends meet.

I knew beyond a shadow of doubt that the Lord had sent me there specifically to interpret her dream. As I checked out at the counter with my new phone charger I asked her about her dream. She told me the dream as if we had been friends forever. It was clear to me what the dream meant, and I told her what I saw in the dream. She was blown away! After I told her the interpretation, she said, "It all makes sense now," and she proceeded to tell me another dream she had recently.

Again, the Lord gave me a clear interpretation for her dream. She was utterly amazed and fascinated. The two definite interpretations left her speechless and all her co-worker could manage to say was, "You must be a pastor or something."

Walking to the van, I wondered why I had not invited them to the services that night. The Holy Spirit informed me that I was not sent there to invite them to church, but to interpret her dreams. We have to be careful to walk in the spirit and to not depend upon our religiosity. I have found that once we have the anointing figured out it has become religion to us.

The Lord having me there with no one else around, just to interpret her dreams, was like Him saying to her, **"Can you hear me now?"**

There is Nothing Wrong with Doing Nothing

Several years back I had a team in New Orleans for a weekend of street ministry. There were fifteen in our team and we were staying at a rental house in the French Quarter on this particular trip. After we had gotten our room assignments and stored our luggage, it was time for the team to meet in the living room. This would be the time when we would get the instructions of where we would be going and when we would depart.

The problem was, I was the guy who was to give these instructions and I had none to give! I had no direction from the Lord as to where we would be going. To make matters worse, everyone was relying upon me. There they sat, staring at me as if to say, "Well?"

I was totally blank which is very uncommon for me. I am the type of person for whom it takes more faith to *not* do something than it does to *do* something. In other words, I am a lot better at moving and shaking than sitting and waiting.

I was getting a little unsettled, and a bit uncomfortable, not having something to say, when all at once, the Holy Spirit spoke to me: ***"There is nothing wrong with doing nothing if anything you do of yourself is nothing anyhow."*** I had to think a moment on that one. It seemed like a riddle or something to be solved.

I then realized, not even Jesus could do anything of Himself that would amount to anything eternal. He even said it Himself: "I can do nothing of myself." But He only did that which He was shown or told of the Father (John 5 and 15).

I got it. There was no leading of the Lord, so there was no need to do anything. Anything I did of myself would only amount to nothing, it would be unfruitful.

It was as soon as I "got it" that I went into an open vision. In this vision I could see a jukebox playing a familiar song, Jimmy Buffet's "Margaritaville." Now I was really wondering what was going on! Could God really use a secular song to speak to me? Was I really in a vision? So many questions were going through my mind, and they all seemed to be working against me.

All of a sudden it made sense to me. There is a bar in the French Quarter called Margaritaville, which is owned by Jimmy Buffet. I now knew the Lord was leading me to that area.

As soon as I hit the point of realization, a hand, stretched out from heaven and pushed a button on the jukebox. Mind you, I am still in a vision. The song selection was another Buffet song that I was familiar with from days gone by. The song picked up right at the line that says,

"...it's my job to be picking up the streets. And that's enough reason to go for me."

Just like that, it was over, but I knew I had direction. I was to lead the team into the French Quarter, go to the Margaritaville Restaurant and Bar, and my job was to be doing street ministry. That is how I interpreted the second song. Off we went.

Now I am thinking (to myself), is Jimmy Buffet going to be there? Is he going to be at the bar eating a cheeseburger in paradise with lettuce and tomato, a cold glass of beer, and French-fried potatoes? The Lord had, so far, spoken to me in songs, so was it strange to be thinking the words of the rest of the song. I really did not know what to expect. Prophetic evangelism is like prophecy. What you know you only know in part, and you can only do the part you know. I knew I had part of it, and "He Who began the good work would be faithful to complete it!"

It is important to point out that just as "there is nothing wrong with doing nothing if anything you do of yourself is nothing anyhow," it is vital to know that in prophetic evangelism, one must do what the Lord leads them to do when He leads them to do it. And it must be done in the right spirit. If not done correctly, the ministry will result in nothing. Remember, obedience is simply doing what you are told to do when you are told to do it with the right heart attitude.

We approached the doorway of Margaritaville, and I went in alone. What did I find?

NOTHING!
ABSOLUTELY NOTHING!

There was not a patron in the place. The only person I saw was the bartender, and he never saw me. His back was toward me the whole time. He never once even gazed in my direction. I was now right back where we started. Nothing!

I stepped outside and looked for somewhere to regroup. My team was once again looking at me as to say, "Well, what happened?" I was a bit taken aback and didn't give them any kind of response.

Directly across the street was a small park with some benches and I led the team over to the park. On one side of the park was Decatur Street. On the other side were some small shops. At that time of the day and the season of the year, the shops had already closed. There were a few other small gatherings of people in parts of the park. I was scanning the crowd to see if there were any signs, directions, or leadings of the Lord. Then my eyes saw it.

There, leaning against a park bench, was a broom and a dustpan used for street sweeping.

Now I may have to give some explanation here. The last line of the song the Lord used in the vision was, "It's my job to be picking up the streets, and that's enough reason to go for me." Buffet wrote that song about a street sweeper in Key West. Now the Lord was using it to tell me I was supposed to sweep the park with the broom and dustpan across the street from Margaritaville in the French Quarter. It was my job. And it was enough reason to *GO* for me. It was time to step into action.

I went straight to the broom and dustpan and began to sweep the park. At that point, the members of the team who were with me started to pick up debris. This led to various conversations with the other people resting in the area. One group was some homeless teens, just sitting on the brick pavers of the courtyard. A few members of our team engaged in conversation with them. They were stranded with nowhere to stay, and, at that point, nothing to eat, so a few of our team went to purchase some meals.

Another group, as I recall, was a few women from Mississippi who were in town for a shopping spree. They had just shopped until they were about to drop. While resting on the benches, they saw me sweeping and the team joyfully cleaning the park. They asked me what we were up to and I told them that we were there for the weekend to do street ministry, sharing the love of Christ. They immediately came under conviction of the Holy Spirit and began to confess their sinfulness. They each prayed to surrender their hearts to Jesus!

The meals then arrived and the team was able to share the gospel with the homeless teens. Some of them prayed to receive Christ as well!

It was amazing to see what a little act of obedience would come to. The truth is that without a vision the people will perish. Could that mean that when we have a vision and obey it, people will get saved?

Now I realize that sometimes people question whether God can really speak like that, using old, secular songs to get His point across. Can He? Yes! He is God!

"Why does He speak like that?" may be the next question. I don't think it is as much about God as it is about the person to whom He is speaking. He speaks to us in ways we can understand. Everyone who knows God hears Him speak in his or her own dialect. It only seems right that He would speak to each of us in our own intellect as well.

Annie and Margret's

Our ministry offices were strategically located in the inner city of Huntsville, Alabama. There were hundreds of ministry opportunities within walking distance on any given day. It was a great place to be for a ministry with a vision to help the poor. A lot of people get discouraged, and some eventually get out of the ministry because they do not see any evident change soon enough. I have learned that if you can't heal them, at least help them. Ministry to the poor is a truly compassion based ministry that takes a lot of endurance and long suffering. If you keep doing what you know to do, God will eventually show up and do the things only He can do! Keep your mind on helping to bring change *to them*, not *it*. In other words, help the poor and don't try to abolish poverty. As Jesus said, "The poor you will always have with you." We will never eradicate poverty but we can help erase fear, doubt, hopelessness, and a few hunger pangs.

While occupying this location in the inner city, I became acquainted with many of the area residents. There were two elderly ladies in particular that I became especially fond of. Margaret and Annie were their names. Margaret was well into her seventies and Annie well into her eighties, but I am not too sure they knew exactly when they were born. To the best of their recollections, Annie was about eight or ten when Margaret, her niece, was born. Annie could remember the a big portion of the 1930s, but Margaret could only remember a little bit of them. That was how they figured their age. They had lived together for quite some time. Both widowed and with all their siblings having passed on, they nestled together in an old, dilapidated house. Their main source of heat was a wood burner in which they burned scrap two-by-fours from the local lumberyard. The floors were so warped you could not close the bathroom door to walk into the kitchen. It was a terrible sight to behold. I could only imagine what it would be like to live in those conditions.

As we were moved in our hearts with compassion for these two, we looked for every opportunity we could find to better their circumstances, like fixing the caving-in porch roof and repairing parts of the floor. Without a doubt, both Annie and Margaret appreciated the repairs. However, they appreciated more the times we would take the time to sit and visit. It was at one of those visits that Margaret said she was not feeling well. Immediately, I was prompted to ask if I could pray for her, and she readily accepted. As I reached out to pray for her, I heard the Lord tell me to pray for her rheumatoid arthritis to be healed and cause her no more pain. I did as I was told. Her response after the amen was, "How did you know? The doctor said I had arthritis and it was here to stay. I don't feel it anymore!" I did not know what the doctor said but only what the Great Physician told me.

Through the years we were in that neighborhood, we would host teams of teenagers who would come to serve in evangelism and service oriented projects. They would come to us from all over the United States. It was one of these groups that painted Annie and Margret's new porch. They did not just get to help Annie and Margaret, but they also got to know them. In the summertime, the front porch is where Annie and Margaret spent their days.

A few years had passed since that summer when Margret's arthritis had been healed and the new porch had been freshly fixed and painted. One of the out of town youth that had helped work on the porch came for another visit. Jessica was her name, and she asked if we could go and visit Annie and Margret. As we pulled up at their house, it was obvious they already had some visitors. There was a woman in her thirties and a young boy who seemed to be about twelve years old there. They were in conversation on the front porch.

I approached the porch near enough so that Margret could recognize me and she piped up and said, "There's the Preacher now—the one I told you about who prayed for me and I was healed." Then she told her guest, "You need to let him pray for you now."

I found out the lady was dealing with a terrible headache. As soon as she said, "Would you please pray for me?" the Lord spoke to me to turn around, pick up this young boy, lift him toward heaven, and pray these words. Before I tell you the words I was to pray, you need to understand a few things.

This "little" boy probably weighed at least 160 pounds! There was nothing little about him. What I was hearing from God, mixed with my thoughts, sounded something like this "pick up that one hundred and sixty pound boy, whom you don't know, and pray this prayer over him—instead of praying for the woman's headache."

Without hesitating, I did what I was told. Let me throw in something here about obedience—obedience is doing what you are told to do, when you are told to do it, with the right heart attitude. It may not always be what you want to do; obedience is not merely based upon what you are doing. In Christianity, it is solely based upon the Person for Whom you are doing it. Now mind you, I picked him up but it was not very far off the ground.

When I picked up the boy and looked toward heaven, I spoke in an audible voice something like this: "Lord, I hold this young boy up to you and thank You that You are watching over every aspect of his life, and that you are protecting him from the abuse and rejection of his mother. You, Lord, have a plan for his life to prosper him."

Here I am, supposed to be praying for the mother's headache, and I am boldly stating that the mother is abusive and has been neglecting the boy. While I am praying this prayer, I am thinking along these lines: 'Headache! That is what I am about to get when this mother hears what I am saying. She is going to whack me upside my head!'

When I finished the prayer and set him down, I could hear the mother crying. Now I thought, "I have hurt her feelings." She looked up to me and asked, "How did you know that?"

At that point I did not have an answer, but she continued, saying, "I have been so stressed out, wondering if I had done the right thing. I just adopted him yesterday because his mother had been abusing him and had abandoned him just recently."

Then she said, "My headache is gone!"

I am an Atheist

One of my all time favorite places to go and minister is in Orange County, California. One of my closest friends planted and is the pastor of a great Church in Huntington Beach, California called the Sanctuary. If you ever get a chance, you need to check it out. I love preaching to the hundreds of souls there that are hungry for the power of God. Quite often, Pastor Jay Haizlip and I get to minister outside of the church as we both have a heart for evangelism.

Pastor Jay is a professional skateboarder who is making a profound impact on the Orange County skate scene and surf culture, not to mention the countless others who just fall in love with Jesus. Because Jay is an avid skater, we often frequent different skating venues, which many times opens doors to meet people and talk to them about the Lord, His saving grace, and the incredible plan He has for their lives.

On one of these many trips, Jay had picked me up at the airport, and we went straight to the Claim Jumper restaurant at the South Coast Plaza. Jay had to meet a young man who was the lead singer for an up and coming punk rock band. He was also just coming to know Jesus in a more personal way and Jay was pouring into him. They were getting ready to play one of their biggest gigs that night. They had a slot at the Viper club in Hollywood right on Sunset Boulevard. This was the club owned by Johnny Depp and also known as the place where River Phoenix died of a drug overdose. It was a very popular club and known as a place for many bands to be discovered.

Before we left the restaurant, both Jay and I agreed we needed to be there that night to show this young believer we loved him. It would be a fun way to do some evangelism, as well. This guy, needless to say, was a bit surprised that two "preachers" would come and visit a punk rocker at the Viper. I think his words were, "Killer, dudes, that's rad."

Well, of course, because it was a club and because they were a punk rock band, their show didn't begin until at least ten o'clock that night, so we had some time to kill before the show. Jay wanted to stop in Long Beach to "drop in" at the skate park. We were very near the neighborhood where Snoop Dog came from. Needless to say, it was not the best of neighborhoods because it was "the Hood." Of course, Jay skated, and I watched. There were not many people there that night, so I was kind of to myself. I started thinking of where we might eat. There are plenty of good places to eat in Hollywood, let alone on Sunset Boulevard. Coming to Southern California from Northern Alabama, I wanted to make the most of my cuisine opportunities.

The Holy Spirit interrupted my thoughts, and I heard him say to me, "You are going to be eating at Subway."

I thought, "Come on. You have got to be kidding me, Subway! You can get Subway anywhere, and if you only knew how many times I have had to eat Subway in my travels because it is the only thing available at late hours. And now I have to eat Subway in Tinsel Town!" God said I was going to eat at Subway. It was just the way it was going to be. I did not say anything to Jay, and I was just waiting to see what was going to happen, and hoping I was not hearing the Lord.

We got to the Viper and found a parking place. Realizing we did not have a lot of spare time before the show, we needed to find something close by. There was only one place to eat that we could see: **Subway!**

It was right across the street from the Viper. As the Lord said, so it was—into the Subway we went. It was close to closing time, and the young man working had pretty much closed shop. I am sure he was ready to go, just as anyone who had made subs all day for someone else would. He had cleaned counters, stacked stools, and taken out the trash. Like I said, he was ready to go, and I do not think he really wanted us to stay, but where else could we go? It is one thing to have to eat at Subway on Sunset Boulevard, but it is a whole different story if you have to eat your sub sitting on the curb!

Jay asked if we could sit in the dining area. He obliged, asking if we didn't mind cleaning up after ourselves. All the tables had been wiped down and all the stools had been stacked. Just as we sat down, in came another customer to order a sandwich. He, too, chose to eat in the dining area.

He was trying to get his stool down to be seated, talking on his cell phone, and holding his bagged sandwich. Although it was obvious to me, he was struggling to accomplish the task at hand, and I heard the Holy Spirit speak to me. "He cannot **manage** his life." Quickly I stood up to help him get the stool off the counter.

Once he finished his phone conversation, he kindly turned in our direction and said, "Thank you. I could not **manage** what I was trying to do." He had just spoken the key word the Lord had given to me. I now knew there was a connection.

Recognizing his foreign accent, I asked him where he was from.

He replied, "Tel-Aviv." He was obviously Jewish. So my straight response was, "Wow, I found your Messiah." To that he was a little startled. As Christians, the Apostle Paul said that we, as Gentiles, would provoke the Jews to jealousy!

Now that the Messiah had been mentioned, he knew what I meant and that I was a Christian. He replied back to me, "I am an atheist."

"So you believe in God!" I replied.

"No, I am an atheist."

"Yes, I know, so you really believe in God."

He said to me plainly, "No, I am an atheist. What about that do you not understand?"

I answered his question with another question. "Let me ask you a question. How can you make a belief system based on something you do not believe exists?"

He looked at me as if he was in deep thought and contemplation, as if to say, "I have never thought of it that way." I must say that I had never thought of it that way either. It was the leading of the Holy Spirit. I could have easily said, "Only a fool says in his heart there is no God, and another word for "atheist" is "fool." I am not too sure how far that kind of conversation would have gone. I know it is written in Scripture that a fool says in his heart there is no God. However, we must keep in mind that the letter kills and the Spirit gives life. If we were to only quote Scripture, we would bring death to those we are trying to get born again. Maybe that is why we have so many stillborn Christians today. All we give them is Scripture, doctrines, and laws but no spirit life. I chose to go the direction the Spirit was leading.

I then proceeded to ask him what his problem was with God. I have come to find that most every self-proclaiming atheist has had a bad experience with someone of the faith, or they have somehow become offended at God Himself for not healing them or keeping someone who was dear to them from danger.

He then went on to tell me his story and to ask me a question.

He had been a young soldier in the Israeli army. All the young residents of Israel were required a period of service in their national army. He and his best friend went to serve their time together. While they were on guard duty in a Palestinian border area on the Gaza strip, his friend stuck his head up out of their foxhole. And as soon as he did, he was shot by an enemy soldier right in the forehead, and fell dead in this young man's arms.

Then he asked me. "Where was your God then?"

My God? I worship the God of the Jews!

"He was in the same place He was when His son Jesus was crucified... on His throne."

This brought conviction to him and opened his heart to where we could pray with him. He actually returned to his faith in God!

Bitter in Houston

During my second visit to Houston, I was strongly impressed by the Lord that I would one day walk the streets of this city. I didn't know at this time, but Houston is the fourth largest city in the United States. The "how" by which I would get there, and even the "when," I didn't know yet. I knew in my spirit man that the day would surely come. That is a prophetic part of evangelism. The Spirit starts to show you what is to come before you ever get there. It is the beginning stages of vision. You see it before you do it.

Once again, the same ministry that helped me get to Portland called me for another engagement. This time, the event they wanted me to speak at was to be in Houston! There is a lot of truth in the saying, "where there is vision there will be provision." I often think about the verse that tells us that Jonah paid his fare to go to Tarshish. I have to wonder if he had gone to Ninevah, like he was instructed, if God would not have paid his fare for him. Now, I am not saying you will never have to pay your way, but I do believe, more often than not, that the Lord will provide for His given work.

On this trip, I was going to be meeting up with the man who had discipled me and taught me the concept of "walking in the Spirit." Phil Smith had been the dean of students at Outreach Ministries of Alabama while I was there. It was there that I noticed Phil had something most professing Christians I had met up to that point did not have—a close personal relationship with the Holy Spirit. For prophetic evangelism, this is a must. If anyone is going to flow in prophetic gifting, they need to be connected to the Holy Spirit Who gives the spiritual gifts "severally as He wills." The more we are doing His will, the more opportunity there is for the gifts to flow.

It is important to mention here that you will gain a great advantage in evangelism if you have been discipled. The great commission, from which we get our forthright command to spread the gospel around the world, tells us to go make disciples. It would be hard to make something that you have not been made yourself! Simply put, we need to be discipled to be able to make disciples.

Upon arriving in Houston, it was not long before I found Phil, who had arrived a few minutes before I had. We were excited about the adventure that lay ahead of us. The first night I had my ministry engagement, and the next night was ours to "take it to the streets." Before we could do that, we needed to know where to go. We made contact with a local church in the inner-city area. They just so happened to have an outreach team that went out on the streets every Saturday night. It was obvious that we should join them.

We spent the better part of Saturday catching up with each other and praying for our ministry that night. It got close to meeting time and we headed for the church to join the others who were going out to minister. The church was located in the Fourth ward—not an area that would normally draw your normal weekend visitor to the great city of Houston, Texas. We pulled up in the parking lot and were the only ones there. After a few minutes, another car pulled in next to us, and out stepped a white haired, seventy-something year old gentlemen. As he walked in front of our vehicle toward the doors of the church, Phil said excitedly, "That's Brother Mep!"

He jumped out of the car and spoke enthusiastically. "Brother Mep, is that you?"

The white-haired man said without even turning around, "Yes, it is me," as if, "Why should anyone be surprised to see me here?"

Brother Mep is short for Brother Meppelink, one of the directors of the Teen Challenge Ministries founded by David Wilkerson. He had been in the national offices, located in Cape Girardeau, Missouri, until he heard that they closed the door of the Teen Challenge in Houston. He felt the burden, packed his bags, and moved to Houston. He was walking the streets of Houston every Saturday night to reach out to young men stranded on the streets (I only hope and pray I have that kind of compassion when I am in my seventies). We knew Brother Mep from his association with the program where I was a student and Phil was a staff member. This encounter stirred in my soul that God was up to something bigger than us.

We waited until about 7:15 to see if anyone else would be joining us. No one else showed. There was a guy who had told Brother Mep he would meet him on the streets, so there were to be four of us that night—Phil and I would minister together, and the other two would be partners. We were off to Montrose Street.

After meeting up with the other guy, we joined hands and prayed together for the Lord to lead us in the right direction and give us His words for those we would meet. They went one way and we went the other with plans to meet at an appointed time right where we had prayed.

We walked and prayed, asking the Lord to guide our path. We turned up one street and, man, did the atmosphere change. It was very dark and had a hostile feel to it. Everyone we walked past gave us strange looks. The bars had unusual activity outside the doors. It just seemed different. Then we realized we were in a predominantly gay district. There were hundreds of men living in homosexuality. To be honest, it startled us. This was the first time I had ever seen this lifestyle so blatantly being lived out in such magnitude. As we went further down this side street, we realized it was not where we were supposed to be. We turned around and headed back toward Montrose.

As we were walking down Montrose, we were approaching a bus stop, and on the bench sat two young guys. Neither of them were talking to each other, but it was obvious they were accompanying one another. As we were passing by, I felt prompted to ask them if they needed a ride. This came to me out of nowhere, which is so often how the prophetic can originate—just as a thought that pops into your mind at a certain moment that can seem incredibly right or awfully wrong.

Again, it is so important to keep in mind that the flesh and the Spirit are contradictory to one another (Gal. 5:17), yet we still have to walk in both of them, (Gal. 2:20). So often what the Spirit will lead you to say or to do is quite opposite of what would make sense in the natural (the flesh). Carnal thinking can challenge hearing the Spirit. Have you ever walked away from someone you were sharing Christ with and said to yourself, "I felt like saying," or, "I should have said," but you did not say it because it did not seem to make sense at the time? More often than not, I have found that it is the Spirit speaking to me, and my carnal nature is resisting. It can be a pretty good indicator as to whether it is from the Spirit or not, if your carnal nature opposes.

For instance, when we came upon the two young guys sitting at the bus stop, on Montrose, I sensed I should ask them if they needed a ride. Logically speaking, of course they needed a ride or they would not be sitting at a bus stop, waiting for a bus.

Furthermore, I was about a mile away from our rental car and had no idea where I would take them, not to mention we had an appointed time to meet the other two men we had joined on the streets. It just did not make sense for me to ask them if they needed a ride, so I kept walking and never said a word. The best way to discern what is of the Spirit or not, is to be mature in knowing His voice.

After about three steps past the bus stop I felt totally stripped naked or bare—not physically, but spiritually. I literally felt like I had just walked out of the Spirit of God as if I was removed from Him. It is important to realize that if one can walk in the Spirit, he can walk out of the Spirit. This really caught my attention, and I realized I needed to turn around and ask those two guys if they "needed a ride," and that is exactly what I did without further hesitation.

Without "hem hawing" around, I straight out asked them the question. Do you guys need a ride? To my surprise, they simply said, "Yes!" They went on to tell us that they had just missed the last bus for the evening and were wondering what they were going to do! Go figure. How was I to know the bus schedule? But the Holy Spirit who knows all things will lead us and guide us into all truth. Keep in mind, the world is groaning for the revealing of the sons of God. Who are the Sons of God? As many as are led, of the Spirit, they are the sons of God. (Romans 8:14) For the Son of God to be revealed we must be Spirit led. It is the Spirit's main function to reveal Jesus.

Going back in the direction we had come from, Phil walked ahead with one of the guys while the other guy and I were behind them. Having some small talk as we walked, the Holy Spirit said to me, "Tell him he has bitterness in his heart." Now, there is a way to get to know someone! For that matter, how would I know he had bitterness in his heart? I had just met the guy minutes before. My thoughts were, "How am I going to tell him that?"

Knowing it was the Lord, and not wanting to miss His promptings, I mused over how to say it. I said, "I believe the Lord wants me to tell you something. He has shown me that you might have bitterness in your heart."

He snapped back at me, **"I don't have bitterness in my heart. What makes you think I have bitterness in my heart?"** He was really mad, and I had obviously struck a chord, or maybe, a root of bitterness!

He calmed down, and as we continued to walk, the Holy Spirit prompted me again, "Tell him he has bitterness in his heart." I thought to myself, as I have many times in such situations, "You tell him! Did you see how he responded to me?" I knew better than that, and I wanted to be obedient to the voice of the Lord. Yet again, I mused over how to go about saying it. The other thought going through my mind was how fast I could duck and dodge being hit by him once I said it.

Once again, I said, "I believe the Lord wants me to tell you that you have bitterness in your heart." Again, he snapped back at me, and he was really angry with me for saying what I said. The conversation was not going really well, and I was thinking twice about giving them a ride. It was obvious by his reactions that he had bitterness in his heart. We continued to walk. We had not gone far and the Spirit did it again:

"Tell him he has bitterness in his heart."

This time, I got it! Simply tell him "You have bitterness in your heart." Do not try to find the politically correct, or theologically correct, way to tell him. Do not hide behind the precursor: "The Lord wants me to tell you...." No, just simply tell him what the Lord is telling me to tell him.

I said, **"You have bitterness in your heart."**

All of a sudden, he burst into tears, sobbing uncontrollably. He fell upon my shoulder as we stood in the sidewalk and just wept. Something was unlocked in this young man's heart. The key was the pure, unadulterated Word of God being spoken to him as if the Lord Himself would have said it—with authority. That is something we as believers are lacking today—the authoritative word of God speaking as one who has authority and offering life to those whom we speak.

After he gained some composure, he told us what had happened in his life to let bitterness set into his heart. His mother was a Christian missionary to parts of Mexico. She was very enthusiastic and devoted to her work. She would often leave her children at home when she would go to visit churches to raise support for her missions. One Sunday afternoon, he and his little sister were at home waiting for their mother to return from church. They were twelve and eight years old. Their mother had told them she would come straight home from church and take them out for a picnic.

This is something she had said many times before, but had not kept her word. Her work was more important to her than keeping her word to her children. As the day moved on, his mother did not show up at the time she said she would. It was now an hour later and still no sign of Mom. His little sister said, "Well, since she is not coming home again, I am going across the street to play at the park." Off she went, but she never made it across the street. A car hit her and she lay dead. Right before his eyes lay his little sister who had once again been let down by their mother.

The very next car to come down the street pulled into their driveway. It was their mother. She was only an hour late. This time she was seconds late. From that moment on, he had resentment toward his mother for his sister's death. I could not blame him for his feelings toward his mother. God knew better, and if that root of bitterness and spirit of unforgiveness were not taken care of, the root would spring up and defile many, and the unforgiveness would keep his own sins from being forgiven.

As soon as he finished telling us his story, Brother Mep and his friend met up with us. We shared with them what had just taken place—the young man had just given his life to Christ and had forgiven his mother. Brother Mep asked him, "What are you going to do now?"

His reply was that he did not know what to do next. He needed a job. The man with Brother Mep said, "What kind of work can you do?" He said he could do irrigation installations. The other guy told him he owned an irrigation business, and he could start working for him on Monday. "But I don't have anywhere to live."

"That's alright," said the man. "You can live in the apartment above the workshop and have it as part of your pay."

"Well then," said the boy, "I just need a church to go to."

His new employer said, "You can come to church with me," and off they went to his new home with his new job and his new church. We did not even have to give him a ride. The Lord did not say to give him a ride. He said, "Ask them if they need a ride." Before we went to the airport the next morning, we stopped by that little inner-city church. Guess who was at the front door, helping give out bulletins? That's right! It was the boy who used to have bitterness in his heart.

Not only was he greeting at the door, he later went out with the church bus to help bring children in from the neighborhood. I have always believed that when someone has encountered Christ, they will want to tell others. He had obviously had that encounter.

NYC

Gretchen and I had been to New York City before, but never with a team. Our first trip originated with me coming home from a day of dealing with a lot of people who had issues—you know trivial church issues. I was their pastor so I got to hear it all. When I got home that day, I told Gretchen I needed to get away from people. She asked me where I was going. "New York City," I said. Her response was, "Can I go with you?"

I remember hearing the late David Wilkerson, the author and main character in the "Cross and the Switchblade." He was also the founder of Teen Challenge Ministries, a worldwide faith based drug and alcohol rehabilitation. And he was also the founding pastor of the soul wining Times Square Church in downtown New York City. He said that whenever he found his heart growing cold or indifferent toward lost souls he knew it was time to take a walk in the streets of the city. There he would encounter the lostness of man and experience the pain and suffering of those stranded on the streets. It would not take long for the mercies of God to stir the compassion for souls once again. I knew it was time for me to take a walk!

The last place anyone would want to go to get away from people would be NYC. There are over eight million people who live in that area. There are people everywhere. Gretchen knew what I had meant by what I said. I needed to get away from everyday church culture. I needed to get in the streets and make contact with the lost. I felt New York would be a great place to do so. That is how we initially got to NYC.

While on this trip, we came upon a homeless man sitting on the busy sidewalk, holding a sign in his hands with a cardboard box in his lap, hoping to get some donations. Many of us have seen the signs homeless people will use to generate funds:

"Will Work for Food"

Well, this sign read, "Cuss me out for a dollar." I was startled, stunned, shocked, and caught off guard. I had just seen someone talking to him as we walked up, and they walked away laughing after putting a dollar in his box and cursing this man who, just like them, had been made in the image of God.

Without hesitation, I felt the leading of the Holy Spirit to give him a five-dollar bill. I reached in my pocket and squatted down in front of him. As soon as I did, some people stopped to hear what I was going to say, as if they wanted to be entertained by my cussing out a homeless man. I started to speak directly to him and loudly enough to be heard, saying that he was wonderfully and beautifully made and marvelous are the works of God. I went on to say that he was fearfully made in the image of God, and that God's thoughts for him are to prosper him and give him a hope and a future. With many other words, I exhorted him. As I spoke, the crowd realized that I was not cussing, but blessing him. They were disappointed and walked away. My heart was grieved for this man and those he represented, not to mention all of those who take pleasure in verbally abusing him.

After that trip, I knew we needed to take a team with us to walk the streets and minister to the multitudes of souls who we had witnessed wandering aimlessly in the streets. Whether they were wearing well-tailored suits or shredded rags, they were like dead men walking. Although you may be inches away from thousands of people walking in Times Square or sitting side-by-side in crowded subways, you never really feel connected or close to them. Seldom do you ever even get to make eye contact. It was, or I should say, it *is* as if no one wants to let anyone in his or her life. That is why we returned with a team to do some prophetic evangelism.

The team we formed not only consisted of the team of young adults who we had been discipling, but we also had along with us our six young children. Spencer, who is our oldest child, could not have been more than nine or ten years old. It was going to be quite a challenge to not only do NYC, but to have to navigate it with six children ages ten and under. Nevertheless, we had a mission to accomplish, which was getting life to the lifeless.

In team preparation before we went to NYC, I asked everyone to pray and ask the Lord to give him or her a word or vision regarding our time in the Big Apple.

After some time in prayer, I asked if anyone had heard or seen anything from the Lord. Only one guy raised his hand. He told us that he had had a vision of our team being under distress in Times Square and becoming very vulnerable, but that while we were in that situation, one of us would see someone they knew right there on the street. It was to be a sign that everything would be okay and that God knew right where we were.

While we were in the city, trying to get adjusted to the large crowds and city layout, we became separated from two of the guys on our team. That was bad enough, but to top it off, they had two of our children with them!

You must understand. We had a few cell phones, but there was not the technology there is today to provide good reception. We had no way of contacting them!

There the rest of the team stood, wondering what we should, or even could, do to rectify the situation. To say the least, it was getting a little stressful.

After many unsuccessful attempts to reach the separated team members by phone, we even tried to re-track a few of our steps, sending a few members back some blocks as we waited for them to return. We were now pretty much exasperated in our efforts and ideas. I had the team gather together to pray for divine intervention. Just as we were getting ready to pray, we heard someone shouting, "Jackie, Jackie!" This man was crossing the intersection where we were gathered. He was quickly approaching us, still saying "Jackie! Jackie!"

I think the only person on our team who seemed to not notice the man calling out for Jackie *was* Jackie, who was one of our team members! She was an exchange student from Nairobi, Kenya, who was spending her summer interning with our ministry. She was not really thinking that someone in New York City was going to be calling her by name. Not only were the odds against it since she was from Kenya, but the school she attended in the States was in Pulaski, Tennessee. The small town of Pulaski has a population of seven thousand people. The school probably did not even enroll as many as five hundred students. Of all the people on our team, she was the least likely of any of us to see someone she would have known. Is that not just like God?

Remember the vision. (We would have someone see one of us in our time of distress, and it would be God's way of letting us know everything was going to be okay)? The gentleman who knew Jackie was a pastor in Pulaski, and Jackie had only been to his church once! We prayed together, asking him to agree with us for the present need.

The closing word in prayer is most often, "Amen," appropriately so, as it simply means "so be it." As sure as we said amen there came our lost team members and our two sons!

Now we knew we were there for a reason and that God was with us, but we still did not know where to go to minister. I felt the Lord prompting me to lead the team to the nearest coffee shop. Now that may seem common to you—a good place to sit down and rest with a tasty refreshment but not me. I don't drink coffee and it's just not my "cup of tea" to sit around a coffee shop. Now here I am, and the Lord is leading me to a coffee shop for the team to relax. They all knew how I felt. To say the least, they were excited for the break, but, I must add, a little shocked.

I kept saying to the Lord under my breath, "Lord, I really need to know this is You."

I was very relieved when we walked in the store and they were playing Christian music. That gave me a confirmation that we were in the right place.

There were not enough seats inside to accommodate all of our team, so a few of us went outside to sit on the sidewalk in front of the shop. One of our guys outside had his guitar with him and another had his djembe. They decided to start playing some worship songs right there on the sidewalk. I might add that you never know how or when the Lord is going to use you in someone else's life. For you musicians, it is always important to have your instrument—your gift—with you.

We had only been worshipping for about five minutes when along came two beautiful girls and one very handsome young man. They were all three dressed in black and white. They really looked sharp, and I mean, they *really* caught your eye.

Their natural beauty may have caught our attention, but it was amazing to see how our worship caught their attention. All at once, the three of them stopped dead in their tracks. They had just stepped into the presence of God and immediately joined in the worship, singing the words right along with us. They were actually captivated with the presence of the Lord there on the streets in front of the coffee shop. Tears were now rolling down their cheeks. Their lives were being impacted.

After a few songs, we were asked to stop playing music on the sidewalk because it was causing a crowd to gather. It was then that some of our team members got a chance to introduce themselves to our three guests. They were in town for a Christian Models Convention. They definitely met the criteria for being models. It was also obvious they had some Christian involvement in their lives, since they knew all the songs we were singing, but, what about their convention? They told us they were actually sneaking away from the convention because it was boring and that they were going to go out and do a little "night life" in the city. They had actually planned to go to some clubs to dance and drink the night away. However, they walked right into the presence of some young adults who were embracing the presence of God on the streets. They immediately were convicted and led into His presence. They knew the Lord had led us there to keep them from going where they were headed.

They were absolutely amazed…yes, amazed by His grace— a grace that teaches us to say "no" to ungodliness and worldly lust. (Titus 2:11) These guys were walking away from their heavenly purposes and convictions of the Holy Spirit and being led by the lust of the flesh but right then and there, in that small window of time the Holy Spirit interrupted them. Intercession means to fill the gap, God is looking for people to fill the gap. Not just praying but putting feet to your prayers. You know what is amazing to me about grace? I do not know how it works; I just know that it does works! It is not as much about knowing the how, it is knowing the Who! I have come to believe that when you have the anointing figured out, it becomes religion and religion does not do the works of grace.

It is by grace we are saved, not just from past sins, but kept from future ones. It is His grace that teaches us to say no to ungodliness and worldly lust. Let me say something about AMAZING grace. His grace gets us through the maze of life. What we cannot figure out, His grace has a way of working out.

The Subway

The first day of our mission trip, our team had been in New York City for a whole day and had yet to minister to anyone. I decided we needed to pray and ask the Lord to more clearly lead us in the way he wanted us to go, and believed there would be someone for us to minister to. No one on our team had a good sense of how to get around the city, being we were from Alabama and found ourselves trying to navigate in the Big Apple. We must have looked like deer staring into headlights. Of all things the Lord could lead us to do, he chose for us to ride on the subway with no specific destination, just a specific line to ride.

Off we went to board the subway, all twenty of us. One detail we had was for us to spread out in different cars, and that is what we did. In the train car with me was one of our guitar players and our djembe player, and both of these guys had their instruments with them. Along with the above mentioned was Jackie, an exchange student from Nairobi, Kenya. We were even a little spread out in the car we boarded, trying to broaden the possibility to meet people we could minister to.

Very seldom in NYC do people make eye contact with each other. It is almost like they do not want to connect with you. Being from the South, where everyone waves at each other whether they know each other or not, this was a little foreign to us and made it a little awkward to start conversations.

Then it happened!

The man sitting across from me made eye contact with me. He was a Jamaican and had a very muscular build. He was well dressed and his head was clean-shaven. He was a bit intimidating to address. It was obvious by his arms, especially by his biceps, that he worked out in the gym on a regular basis. He may have been a body builder, and he made eye contact with me. Without having eye contact, it is hard to engage in a purposeful conversation. It was pretty quiet on this subway car because no one was talking.

When my eyes connected this body builder, I said the first thought that came to my mind. I asked, "Do you want to arm wrestle?", patted my right bicep, and smiled. He looked at me a bit surprised, not as much that I asked him to arm wrestle, but more so that I said anything at all. Then he chuckled and flashed a big grin, and he asked me where I was from and what had brought me to NYC. It seemed very obvious to him that I was not from the city. I told him we were there on a mission trip, reaching out to those the Lord would lead us to. I mentioned that the guys with the instruments were with me and the girl was from Kenya.

Because he was from Jamaica, he was interested in the Caucasian guy carrying a djembe, so he asked, "Can he really play that thing?" I said, "Sure, and not only can he play it, she can dance to it as well, pointing to Jackie. "Do you want to hear him?" He smiled and made a little facial gesture that indicated he didn't know how to answer. Out came the djembe, and he started to play there in the subway car. The acoustics were amazing; they just rolled around. Jackie stood up and started to dance to the rhythm, and the guy with the guitar started to play and sing a worship song with them.

I was able to pray, not arm-wrestle (thank goodness) with my Jamaican friend, and when the train stopped, no one got off! We actually went three stops before anyone got off the train. I looked at the cars in front of us and behind us, and our team members were praying with folks and ministering to them. Finally, at the third stop, someone said, "I have to get off here. I was supposed to get off three stops earlier but did not want to leave!" With that said, a bunch of folks acknowledged that they, too, did not want to get off and had stayed on a few extra stops. The presence of God had filled the subway cars we were in and had captivated the hearts of the folks on them.

It may seem strange to think that all of **that** could happen from just asking a person if they wanted to arm-wrestle. It is not just the words we use, but the heart from which we are using them. From the abundance of the heart the mouth speaks. I wanted to connect with people and get the opportunity to share Christ with them. When Jesus spoke to the woman at the well, he did not approach her with religious jargon or words that seemed super spiritual. No, He made Himself vulnerable and asked her for a drink of water. He actually met her on her conditions. We need to meet people where they are and lead them to where we are going, just as Jesus came to earth where we are and leads us to Heaven where He is now. We do not need to be afraid to make ourselves vulnerable. It is important not to intimidate those we are reaching out to. Be humble because by humility we receive grace, and it is by grace that people are saved.

We do not have to open our conversations with lost folks by using Christian terms or Bible quotations. Remember, they are lost or fallen away from the Lord and the church. It would either be nonsense or possibly offensive to them. We need to hear the Lord and be sensitive to how we approach the lost.

By no means is this to say that we would never use a Scripture or a Christian term to engage in a conversation. It is just to emphasize that we must say what the Lord is giving us at that very time—knowing where to meet them so we have a better chance at them meeting Christ.

Happy Valentine's

It was going to be a multipurpose trip to New Orleans. One, we were going to visit Cara, who had recently moved to the city to spend time interceding and serving in the inner city. She had been on many, if not all, the mission trips we had taken as a team. Now she was living out something the Lord had laid upon her heart. Needless to say, I was proud of her and very excited about our visit.

Secondly, I had Salome with me, who is our fourth child. She and Cara have a very close relationship and had not seen each other in quite some time. It was also Salome's birthday, and it was a special gift to her. For the most part, the plan was to just spend some time together......at least that was my plans. I am gaining more and more understanding of familiar Scriptures from the Bible as they are played out right before my eyes, like the Proverb that says, "Who knows the plans of the Lord but the Lord Himself?" How about this one? "Man plans his ways in His heart but the Lord directs his steps." I had no clue what lay ahead of us.

The flight to New Orleans was nothing out of the ordinary. They called for some rain in the area, but it is normal to have afternoon showers in coastal regions. We landed on time and were shuttled over to the rental car office. Once I was in line, I started to experience some severe stomach cramps. I had to leave the line I had been waiting in for close to thirty minutes. I felt terrible leaving Salome waiting alone, but I had no choice.

I returned to the line to check out our vehicle and get on our way. As soon as we stepped across the threshold of the door from the office to the parking lot, lightning struck! It not only struck, but it went right over Salome's head. She was in front of me, and she is a good bit shorter than I am, so what was right over her head was right in front of my face. I could feel the electricity and the brightness was near blinding. I was startled. Actually, everyone in the building was startled. I turned around and saw all the employees wide-eyed, staring at the two of us. As quickly as it struck of course it was gone, but it had started to down pour. It was like a monsoon. We could hardly see twenty feet in front of us. Not wanting to waste any more time, we ran to the car and loaded up to head out.

As we were ready to pull out, there was a gasoline delivery truck leaving the lot. I pulled in behind him and followed him out the gate. The rain was still so heavy, I was just following the lead of his taillights. I felt a little bump while pulling out of the lot but nothing really definite. I heard no scratch and certainly could not see anything around us. Everything felt fine until we were about a mile down Airline Highway. It felt like I was losing the power steering and I had to really struggle to steer the car. I pulled over into a parking lot to make a better assessment. Boy, was I surprised at my discovery! We had four flat tires! That's right!! All **four** tires were flat on a brand new rental car. Of course the sun had come out, and we were sitting in bright daylight at rush hour. We were a funny sight for those in traffic going home from work. Have you ever seen a brand new car with four flat tires?

As I was following the tanker truck out of the lot, I was not aware of the crossbar that did not have time to close. It was raining so hard I could not read any signs. Then later I realized the clerk had never given me a ticket to leave the lot by inserting it at the gate. I had no forewarning of what I was entering into. I was blinded, and now I was sidetracked, and literally, sitting on the side of the road. All I could do now was call the 800 number in my lease agreement. Precious Salome was sitting there not saying a word. Of course, I was a little upset and a good bit embarrassed. Then she said, "Maybe we ought to pray." From the mouth of babes! Oh to have childlike faith. So, we prayed, asking the Lord to see us through the mess.

I reached the customer service department. The person on the other line was actually in New York. "New York, and I am in New Orleans!" Now, keep in mind, I was only one mile from where I rented the car and I was trying to explain to someone in New York where I was stranded in New Orleans. Did I mention I was one mile away from the rental office? This seemed impossible; I was even double guessing, "Am I even supposed to be here?" Finally, they located a wrecker service to come and tow us in. I had to inform the customer service representative it could not be just any tow truck; I had four flat tires.

During the two-hour wait for the tow truck to tow us back to the car lot, which I might add was only one mile away. We had a lot of time to pray, but I did not feel like praying a whole lot until it dawned on me that I did not get the full coverage insurance. Now I had something to pray about! I really did not feel I was to be fully responsible for the tires. I had not been given the ticket, and the weather conditions were way out of my control. Even the people at the counter experienced that with me. I could see no way out of the situation, other than me paying the thousand plus dollars—or rely on the Lord to intervene. My faith was not there yet, and I was still a little confounded. I simply prayed, *"Lord, I do not have that kind of faith right now. I need to tap into your faith and allow you to handle the matter."*

Needless to say, when the tow truck driver pulled up, it was obvious that he wanted to laugh. Come on! Four flat tires? Wouldn't you want to laugh? I told him to go ahead and laugh; I would think it was funny too...one day. Salome had not thought that she was going to get a tow truck ride on this special birthday trip. Hey, who knows the plans of the Lord? Within minutes, we were pulling into the same lot I pulled out of a few hours earlier. It was only a mile ride. That still baffles me.

The woman at the counter was all business and by the law of the book. I am not saying that is wrong, but she acted like she didn't even remember me. She had it in her mind I was going to pay for this ordeal one way or another. I, on the other hand, was standing my ground, believing in God to step in and get me off the hook of paying a bill I felt was not altogether mine to pay. This interchange went on for fifteen to twenty minutes, with neither of us budging. Then it was as if it was time for her to clock out and go home. Without saying a word, she turned and went to the back wall, punched out her time card, and I never saw her again. I was really glad it was time for her to clock out.

Within a few minutes, out walked a sweet-spirited and joyful woman. She said, "Honey, what can I do for you today?" I briefly told her the story. She smiled and said, "Sign here, and here are the keys to a new car." Seriously? Where did she come from? How could it be that easy after being so difficult? I looked down at her nametag. It read *Faith!* Somehow I had just tapped into God's faith, the faith I did not have for the moment. We were on our way.

It was great to see Cara and to catch up on all she had been experiencing while living in New Orleans. After getting settled in, we got ready to walk into the French Quarter to have dinner. We enjoyed the walk and had a nice time together at dinner, as well. After dinner, we decided to make a stop at the famous Café Dumonde for some beignets and a hot choco-late. Afterward, I was ready to head back to the place where we would be spending the night. As we were leaving the café, it was obvious to Salome that we were not going out on the streets to minister. Much to her surprise, she asked me where we were going. I told we were returning to our accommodations to get some rest. With great concern in her voice, she replied, "But we haven't shared Jesus with any on the streets yet." I must say, I was convicted!

We turned around and went into Jackson Square, looking for people with whom we could "share Jesus."

After about an hour or so in the square, it was obvious that Salome was now growing tired, and we had shared Jesus with a few homeless, who themselves were getting ready to bed down for the night. Strangely enough, I now felt there was something or someone else that needed to be attended to. So I accompa-nied the girls' home and returned to the French Quarter to seek out my mission. I have always been inspired by the purpose of Jesus in which He stated and was recorded by Luke in the nineteenth chapter and the tenth verse—He came to "seek and to save the lost." I was now seeking for someone who was lost.

I was walking down Bourbon Street when, out of nowhere, a fight broke out right in front of me. It was not like other fights I have seen and I eventually stepped in to break up. This was different. It was a coed group fight. There were five girls and two guys and it was girls against guys. I am totally unaware of what caused the brawl to break out and I was not even aware, at first, that it was gender against gender. I just knew it would be better for everyone if it were brought to a peaceful order. Without thinking twice, I stepped in to bring order.

That is when I realized it was girls against guys, and that I was, obviously, a guy. My initiation to the brawl was a full cup of beer thrown in my direction. Now, soaked in beer from my face to my waist, one of the girls told me to stay out of it while they were taking it to the guys. I realized I had just stepped into something out of my own will, meaning I was not led of the Lord to engage in this certain matter. Furthermore, I was without covering, leaving myself open to personal harm. I quickly removed my beer-splattered self from the whole ordeal.

I still knew I was not finished for the night. It was there that I prayed, "Lord, lead me to the place or the person you need me to speak. I will go where you go and walk in your Spirit." Without hesitation, I sensed the leading of the Lord to go down one block and take a left. After turning left and getting about halfway down the block, I heard the pitter-patter of someone's steps approaching me from behind. It was almost as if they were running directly toward me. Having just recently had beer thrown in my face, I chose not to turn to see this person approaching me.

Once the sound of the steps got within a few feet of me, just off my right shoulder, the voice of the steps addressed me. He began to say, "Excuse me, sir, can I...." Just as soon as he had started, he stopped in mid-sentence and redirected his address. This time, he looked into my eyes, being only an arm length away, and said, "This isn't about bumming change, is it?"

"No, this is not about bumming change. This is about your life being changed so that you can reach your God-given destiny," was my reply, without even thinking twice. I was as surprised as he was. It is about getting you off these streets and back to your family where you belong. He said, how did you know I was stranded here and separated from my family? Remember, I had just chosen to "walk in the Spirit." This man, in essence, had just walked *into* the Spirit of God because I was walking *in* the Spirit of God.

I spoke with him for a few more minutes and determined to meet him there in Jackson Square the next day. If he were to meet me then, I would know he was serious about wanting to help to get back where he belonged. He was one of many who had become stranded in the "Big Easy."

Getting to know Jimmy and his story, it became evident to me why and what had happened to me upon my entry to the city. The enemy was trying to keep me out of the city so that he could keep Jimmy in the city. Breakdowns precede break-throughs!! Jimmy had come to New Orleans from Mobile, Alabama, to do some work. He was going to make some money and then return home to his wife and children. The only problem was that he lost the job and became stranded in the Big Easy. His car broke down, and lost his apartment. Under all the pressure, he began to drink and could not stop. He was now one step away from being homeless. This was his last night staying in the hallway of the apartment complex. When we met each other in the French Quarter, he had been bumming change to get his next drink. It was easy for Jimmy to get into New Orleans, since New Orleans is the Big Easy. Now it had become almost impossible for him to get out of the city and back to his family. "With man these things are impossible, but with God all things are possible." Walking in the Spirit brings God on the scene!

When we got to the Cathedral the next day, Jimmy was already there with a smile on his face that showed great expectations. From there we went by the apartment complex to get his duffle bag full of belongings and off we went to the bus station to get him out of the Big Easy. It was not more than two hours and we were waving goodbye to Jimmy as he rode off on the bus. It is always challenging to believe everything is going to turn out the way you hope, once it is no longer in your scope. I really hoped Jimmy would make it back home. I hoped he was not just scamming me for a ticket and that he even had a family in Mobile. Sometimes when you are doing prophetic evangelism you realize how true it is that the "Spirit and the flesh are contrary to one another." I knew all along while ministering to Jimmy it was what the Lord wanted me to do, but at the same time, in my natural mind I was wondering, "Is this for real?"

We returned home the same day that we watched Jimmy ride off on the bus. Many times, thereafter, I thought about him and our encounter that night in the French Quarter. I was really struck by the fact that, if I walk in the Spirit, those who walk into me will encounter the Spirit. For that matter, whatever spirit we are in is what others will encounter when they walk where we are. If you are mad, people tend to know you are mad. I was excited to find a new realm of revelation that not only will the Spirit lead **me** into truth, but also when others come into contact with me, they, too, will be in contact with Him!

Over the next few weeks, I shared this with a few friends; one in particular was our pastor's wife. Not long after that she was ministering on a Wednesday night at our church. It was actually February 14th, Valentine's Day. Gretchen and I were going to church and then slip away for a quiet dinner together. We were seated in the back of the church enjoying the service, when all of a sudden Pastor Leisa called for me to come to the stage. I had no earthly idea where she was going! Actually, I was thinking she was going to do some kind of illustration to make a point in her message, but I was caught off guard.

Once I reached the stage, she asked me to share the story of what had happened to me on my recent trip to New Orleans. It had been about three weeks since we had returned and maybe a week since I had told her the story. I proceeded to tell the story about what I had experienced and about how we all can walk in the Spirit and help set an atmosphere for others to experience God. All along I knew it was a great story, yet I was still wondering what became of Jimmy. I love the encounters, but I want the results. It seems like more times than not, we never get to see the fruit of our labors. That is another reason we must walk by faith and not by sight.

After service, walking to the car to take my bride to dinner for Valentine's, we were talking about how interesting it was to have been called up in the service to share the story about Jimmy. When we got in the car I noticed I had a voicemail on my phone from an unknown number. I listened to the message, which was as follows:

"Hi, Greg. I hope you are doing well. I wanted to call and wish you a Happy Valentine's Day, and to say that I love you! This is Jimmy Johnson! I would not be home today with my wife and children if it were not for you and the Lord Jesus Christ! All is well."

He was leaving this voicemail while I was sharing his story in the church. Wow! This Valentine message was from the Lord! He surely is an amazing God!

Would You Like to Play?

In Las Vegas I was helping train some YWAM students on how to operate in prophetic evangelism. One of the student's names was Ted. He really took a liking to the idea of being prophetic while doing evangelism. He was ready to go, inspired by the various testimonies I had given during the lecture week. One thing I always emphasize is to make sure and be yourself. In other words, do not try to be someone or something you are not. Human instinct lets people know upfront whether what you are saying is something you believe in, or whether you are just saying what someone else has said.

We were on Fremont Street and a few of the team started to play Hackie Sack. If you are not familiar with that game, it is the little sock ball that is not much bigger than a golf ball. The players stand in a circle and use their feet to keep the Hackie Sack going without hitting the ground. I must say, it looks fun, but I have yet to participate. Needless to say, I was a spectator, and next to me was an elderly man leaning upon his cane. He, too, was just a spectator.

All of a sudden the Hackie Sack flew out of the circle and landed at the feet of the man next to me who was leaning on his cane. Ted broke from the circle to retrieve the Hackie Sack. As he approached the man, he quickly asked him if he wanted to play. The man next to me laughed and said, "Yeah right," all the while holding out his walking cane.

Remember, this is a game of balance, agility, and all the time, using your feet. Why on earth would Ted ask a man with a cane to play Hackie Sack?

I had taught that week using the story about the man on the New York subway who I had felt the Lord lead me to ask him if he wanted to arm wrestle. It was quite obvious this man would hands down take me in arm wrestling, but it was a great way to start a conversation. When Ted saw that man with a cane, he spoke what came to his mind. Just be yourself and look for opportunities to start a conversation.

Well, Ted went back to the circle, most likely thinking he had just blown it. What he did not realize is that I was looking for a way to get a conversation going with this man next to me. Now we had something to talk about. He turned to me and laughed at what Ted had just asked him, and we began to talk.

As the conversation went on, I realized it was a God-ordained moment. His name was Joe and he had been in Vegas for many years after coming there to gamble. He had become addicted to not just gambling, but also alcohol. He had now been addicted to alcohol for over forty years. He lost his family and everything else he had once owned. He had not seen his children in over twenty years. None of his children had ever seen him sober.

Our meeting extended until late in the evening, we quickly bonded and intended to connect the next night there on Fremont Street. He had no cell phone, so we decided that we would connect there the next evening at a certain time. That sounds easy, but considering the circumstances, it was going to have to be another God encounter. At the time, there could be well over 1.5 million people in the city of Las Vegas. I was working with a team of over thirty young adults from many different nations. It was difficult to get them somewhere by a certain time, not to mention, an alcoholic with a gambling addiction in Las Vegas. who. What would be the odds?

The following evening came and went, and we never saw Joe that night, or the next night, or even the next. We had one night left. Could it be possible? I have to be honest. I had somewhat given up the hope of seeing it happen. If it were to be, then fine, but if it did not happen, fine. By this time I had been away from my family for eleven days, and I was ready to get on the plane and go home! I had been sleeping on a bedroom floor in a sleeping bag all week.

The morning of the last day, while we were in our prayer time, I was approached by Cara. She told me she had a dream the night before of a certain billboard and that she was to find the billboard that night. She asked me if we could be on the same team that night on the streets and look for it. It was, also, in that time of prayer that I felt strong desire to once again see Joe. I knew the Lord had started something and I was now confident that He could finish that good work.

Once we got to the strip on Fremont that night we began our journey. Not knowing exactly where we were going or what we might find once we got there, we just kept praying for the Lord to guide our steps. We took a right turn on one street and a left turn on another, going three blocks, all the time looking for this billboard Cara had seen in her dream.

I honestly cannot remember the path we took to get to where we got. We were most certainly off the beaten path, and there it was, the billboard Cara had seen in her dream! We were practically standing under it. The sign was clear as day since it was lit up at night. We were actually in a darker area of town away from the neon-lighted strips that pulsated and glowed, making everything bright, but I could see the light of His presence in Cara's face once we found the billboard in her dream. Now what? Mission accomplished, or was there a reason the Lord had directed us to this point?

As we stood and wondered, we both saw what the Lord had intended for us to see beyond the billboard. There was Joe, our friend with the cane. He was crossing the street a block away. It was a narrow street, and we saw the tail end of his crossing, and he disappeared into an adjacent casino.

We quickly went to see if we could find him. We slipped into the casino to find a dungeon of cigarette smoke, body odor, and the stench of cheap food. Maybe I sensed the smell of cheap food because of the sign I read as I entered the casino: "Hot Dogs—Two for One Dollar." That is pretty cheap. I must say, I have not been in every casino in Vegas, but of all the ones I have been in, this was the worst of them all. The atmosphere was absolutely depressing.

Joe was waiting in line to get his dogs for a dollar, so Cara and I sided with him in line and I said something to this effect, "Can I buy you a dog or two?" When he turned and saw who it was speaking to him, he looked as startled as we must have looked a few moments earlier when we spotted him because of the billboard we were seeking to find. Go figure!

Maybe he was just so surprised to see us in that particular place. I am telling you, this was no place the tourists would find, and even if they did, they would be looking for the quickest way out of that part of town. The best way I can describe it is that it was the slum of casinos; where the gambling addicts who had lost it all would come to comfort their addictions.

We sat down at a vacant booth to have our dollar dogs. Joe asked the question. "What are you guys doing here and how did you find this place?" I simply told him we were looking for him, that the Lord had led us to the billboard that allowed us to find him. Tears began to well up in his eyes. I really do not think he even halfway grasped the whole "billboard" thing.

However, he was blown away that we, let alone anyone, would be looking for him. The very idea that someone wanted to see him was almost incomprehensible to him. This led into a more personal conversation than we had yet experienced. He revealed that he had purposely kept from seeing us while we were in town. He knew his heart was being drawn to something or someone, but he was afraid. It had been a long time since he had felt this emotional. Love was a stranger to him and something he had not known or experienced in over a generation.

The next day was to be our last night in Vegas. Once again, I had arrangements to meet with Joe. I was going to take him to dinner, along with the leader of the YWAM team. As soon as we entered the Fremont area I saw Joe. He was different. He had shaven and was wearing clean clothes and a smile that made it obvious he was happy and feeling good to be loved.

We went to dinner and what a night it was. At dinner, Joe told us it was the first day he had been sober in over forty years! It was obvious to him that the Lord was after his heart, and he decided to surrender. That's right! He gave his heart to Jesus that day as he contemplated all that had transpired in his life that week.

It was that night after we had finished eating dinner that I loaned my cell phone to Joe to make a call he had not made in years. He called his daughters in Florida. He spoke to a grandchild he had never met, and, again, tears were in his eyes. He then became saddened to hear that his daughter did not want to come to the phone and speak with him, but he did not give up. He understood. She had never spoken to him in all of her life that he was not intoxicated. He was just happy to speak with a grandchild he had not yet met.

Joe's second call was like the first, but better. He reached someone on the other line who was another grandchild. Again, we could see the emotion welling up in his eyes. It was obvious the numbness of heart and soul had been lifted from this old drunkard who had given his life to Jesus. Then his daughter came to the phone. There was great joy in his face and in the sound of his voice, yet still a slight quiver. He had just been rejected from one daughter—might this one do the same?

She was in complete shock and somewhat disbelief. She asked if she could speak with the owner of the phone. She asked, "Is this for real; who are you and what has happened to my dad?" I relayed the story just as I am writing it for you. She was elated and amazed at the grace of God. She was going to call her sister to let her know what an awesome thing had happened to their father, and to hopefully encourage her to accept her dad's call.

As she got back on the phone with Joe, she made an invitation for her dad to come and visit in Florida, at her expense, to reunite with her and to meet the rest of his family for the first time. She was so excited to see the dad she had never seen sober in all her life!

The Preacher's Daughter On Bourbon

Each year, the dates for Mardi Gras change because it coincides with the Tuesday before Ash Wednesday. It can fall anywhere between early February to mid-March. I tend to prefer the mid-March dates for a few good reasons: First, the later we go in the spring, the warmer it naturally tends to be. Even though New Orleans is in the South, it can get pretty cold with the wind coming off the Mississippi River. Spending ten to twelve hours a day on the streets, with intermittent rains, can become quite uncomfortable to say the least.

Second, there is more time to get prepared. When Mardi Gras comes early in the year, it always seems to sneak up on me, having just come out of Holidays and trying to get back in the flow of things. After focusing on the New Year and reminiscing the past, I am not sure about you, but the holidays have a tendency to get me in a spiritual funk. Too much eating and making merry can make a person dull in their spirit man.

Preparation is important for prophetic evangelism. Actually, preparation is important for any operation. One of God's characteristics is preparation. Think about it. Where is Jesus right now? Jesus is in heaven, seated at the right hand of God, and making intercession for us. He is *preparing* a place for us. And King David said that God *prepares* a table for us in the presence of our enemies (Ps. 23:5). One of my favorite passages of all time is 1 Corinthians 2:9:

> *Eye has not seen, ear has not heard, nor has it even entered the heart of man what God has prepared for him.*

We, too, need to be a people of preparation—being ready always to give the answer for the hope that is within us, and being instant, ready to preach the Word, no matter what season we find ourselves. John the Baptist went before the face of the Lord to prepare the way of the Lord. He spent time in prayer with God to get prepared, or to help make preparations, for what God was getting ready to do. This was not just about what God was going to do through John, but through Christ as well. Jesus even taught His disciples the importance of prayer and fasting—to have what it takes to be free from unbelief and to have authority over evil spirits. The more we prepare ourselves in prayer and fasting, the more we will be pre-paired (paired with Christ) to do His will.

Preparation is the antidote for procrastination. Procrastination is putting off what needs to be done. I have come to find out the hard way **that procrastination for the moment can be your best friend, but it will soon become your worst enemy.**

Now it should be obvious why I do not like Mardi Gras to come early. It is harder to get properly prepared, it is less time to spend in focused prayer, and it is certainly less time for fasting!

This was one of those years when it came early and I was not in the spiritual shape or form that I feel an outreach like Mardi Gras requires. Nevertheless, I was there right in the thick of it. We had a good team that year of over 200 evangelists in our camp, which, in most cases, tends to be great. For me, however, it created more to facilitate. I was not even getting time to properly seek the Lord myself due to many needs to address at the camp.

It seems like just yesterday. I had about thirty minutes to pray that morning before I was to preach to the camp to this particular day. I cannot, at all, remember what I preached that morning, or what I had for breakfast, lunch, or dinner, but I can recall, vividly, what I prayed that morning... and what happened that night.

Not having been properly prepared for the outreach, I found myself wrestling with unbelief and, somewhat, doubting my calling. I knew we were there to do evangelism, but I did not feel very prophetic. I even asked the Lord if I was a prophet and to please reveal it to me. There I was, on an outreach to help people to come to know Jesus, and I was wrestling with who I was in Christ.

Now when I say, "Am I a Prophet?" I am not trying to compare myself with Isaiah, Elijah, and Ezekiel in the Bible, but I am relating to the reference to where Moses said, "I would that all the Lord's people were prophets." Joel also prophesied of the great outpouring of the Spirit of God in the last days, when the sons and daughters of God would prophesy. These passages refer to us as the sons and daughters of God who are living in these last days! My prayer was,

"Lord, please show me if I am a prophet."

It must have been ten hours later when I was heading toward Bourbon Street and I said, "Lord, let me see who You want me to see."

As soon as I stepped onto Bourbon Street and took a left, I saw her! She was a blonde, about forty-something, having a really hard time standing up on her own. She was drunk! She was with a guy about half her age. He was Hispanic in descent, holding her up with one hand and holding his beer in the other hand. He seemed to be a bit more concerned about the beer not spilling than her not falling. In a split second, she went down, but the beer was still safe in his hand.

Once she was down, her head went between her legs and she was beginning to pass out. She was on the stoop of the entrance to a beer joint that was no more that a five-by-five hole-in-the-wall that sells what they advertise to be "Huge — Beers." That is all they sell. There is nothing but kegs of beers in there. One of the guys selling the beers was now watching what was taking place. She was on his doorstep hunched over, ready to pass out. Keep in mind; this street is the dirtiest street I know of in the United States of America. It is absolutely nasty, and there she was, sitting in it.

I knew, without a shadow of a doubt, this was whom the Lord wanted me to minister to. I went straight to her and both the beer man and the man with her looked up at me as though they were expecting something to happen. Not only is this a filthy, street, it is a crowded street, especially during Mardi Gras! The crowd can be so large that when you try to cross the street at one block, you can get caught in the crowd and come out a block later! So for these guys to recognize my coming to her was like the disciples questioning Jesus as to say who touched me while a large crowd surrounded them. They just knew I was coming to help.

I asked the young man if I could pray for her and told him I was a minister. He did the "forehead-to-chest-and-across-the-shoulders" thing to me and nodded. I knelt down, put my lips on her right ear, and began to speak the words the Holy Spirit gave me to say.

"Lord, touch her heart today. She has been hurt in so many ways. She is trying to cover up not only the hurt but from the shame of being a Southern Baptist preacher's daughter who was sexually abused when she was twelve and is now away from the Christian faith. Please heal her, Lord!"

Her head popped up and she turned and looked at me with tears in her eyes and said, "How did you know my dad was a Southern Baptist preacher and that I was molested when I was twelve years old? Only God could have known that." She was totally sober! We prayed as she thanked the Lord for healing her and she recommitted her heart to Jesus. This all took no more than four to five minutes.

As I stood up, the guy with her and the beer guy were staring at me, as if to say, "What on earth just happened?" The guy with her did his "Father, Son, and Holy Spirit" thing again and said, "Thank You Father;" as I turned, the beer guy was handing me a cold cup of water. It was not for her, but for me. I took the cup of water and told the other guy to thank the Father above from where all good things flow from.

As I walked away, I thought of the prayer I had prayed that morning and this Scripture came to mind;

"He who receives you receives Me, and he who receives Me receives Him who sent Me. [41] He who receives a prophet in the name of a prophet shall receive a prophet's reward. And he who receives a righteous man in the name of a righteous man shall receive a righteous man's reward. [42] And whoever gives one of these little ones only a cup of cold water in the name of a disciple, assuredly, I say to you, he shall by no means lose his reward (Matthew 10:40-42)."

What's Your Name?

Once again I found myself on the streets of New Orleans. This time, I had a young man with me who was feeling a possible leading to move to New Orleans and minister to those who lived there. He had been with me on other trips to the city, but on this trip, he was hoping for deeper discipleship and, hopefully, more direction on whether or not it was the Lord's will for he and his wife to move there. I was really excited and was hoping and praying the Lord would reveal to him exactly what he needed.

After arriving in the city by airplane, we rented a vehicle and proceeded to the French Quarter, where we were going to be staying. This would give us optimum time on the streets, not having to travel back and forth. We were staying in the St. Louis Hotel. It is located between Bourbon Street and Royal Street. We had been there for one night and were only staying for two before returning home in time for me to preach on Sunday morning. It was Saturday afternoon, and nothing noteworthy had yet happened. I told the young man that I was going to take a walk through the Quarter and see who the Lord may be leading me to minister to. He chose to remain in the Hotel room to spend some time praying in regards to the Lord's will for the future. I went to see where the Lord might be leading.

Coming out of the St. Louis hotel, I headed to my right leading in the direction of the Mississippi River, which is the opposite direction from Bourbon Street. I was simply taking a walk and looking for who it may be that I was to minister to. Granted, there were people everywhere, but there was some-one specific the Lord was leading me to. Not knowing who or where it was that I was going, it required me to be on the look-out. I walked and walked and seemed to never feel the leading of the person with whom I was to connect on this walk.

I had now been gone close to ninety minutes, and was a good twenty-minute walk back to my hotel room. I had still not found that person. I decided to return by way of Bourbon Street. Surely there would be someone on Bourbon (no pun intended) that the Lord would want me to minister to. By the time I reached St. Louis to turn back toward the hotel, I had still not found that person. I was a bit discouraged and disap-pointed. I was thinking maybe I had missed the Lord. I had spent nearly two hours walking the French Quarter and not finding who I felt the Lord had sent me to find.

Then it happened! There he was!

He was no more than fifty feet from the hotel entrance where we were staying... the same doors I had left out of two hours earlier. Sitting on the sidewalk with his back up against the wall was a man eating some food that had obviously been retrieved from a garbage bin. His knees were pulled up to his chest. The cold slop of food lay between his feet. He was unshaven and filthy. It was actually a very pitiful sight. He had not been there earlier; I would have noticed him. This was the person I knew the Lord had sent me to meet; I felt it strongly. I knew I was now in the right place at the right time. The prior two hours did not matter anymore. It was just part of the process.

He had no sense that I had even approached him until I crouched down next to him. His empty, yet steely, eyes made contact with mine. I asked him, "What's your name?" His reply was simply, "What's your name?" To that I replied, "Greg," hoping he might give me his, but that was as far as he went.

I then asked him, "Where are you from?" He asked me, "Where are you from?" "I am from Huntsville, Alabama," I replied.

This was looking like it was going nowhere fast. A sure dead-end... maybe another guy on the streets that had lost all communication skills, but I still knew this was the guy I was meant to minister to. "Do you have any family?" was my next question, and still he displayed no emotion. Although he did stop eating while we talked, he still stared at me with that empty, steely, look. His reply to me was, (yes, you guessed it) "Do you have any family?" Yes, I have a wife and six children." His head tilted a little, which was not uncommon for me when I told people how many children we had been blessed with (at that time).

I thought I would ask one more question. "What did you used to do?" Once again, I was answered with the question I asked; only this time it was a little different. Instead of asking me what I *used to do,* He asked me what I did. It was bringing it into the present and out of the past.

I told him I was a pastor of a church and I was in New Orleans walking the streets, looking for those who the Lord wanted me to meet and share his love and forgiveness. It was at that moment that his eyes started to fill with tears and roll down his cheeks. Something I just said had gotten to him. I asked him if he was okay. This time, he did not ask me a question but answered all my questions.

His name was James. He was from the Huntsville, Alabama area. He had a wife, six children, and he used to pastor a church! Of all the questions I had asked him, only one of our answers was not the same—our names.

As the story unfolded, I had learned that he had been on the streets for the past six years. He had left his family and the church after he had had an affair with one of the women in the church. The shame of the act had led him to start drinking, and the two together led him to leave town without telling anyone. He just up and left.

Needless to say, we were both a little awed at the similarities we held and for him to find out the Lord had sent me to him to remind him he was loved. It just blew him away. After six years of running from it all, the Lord was finding him.

I remembered the young man traveling with me and I wanted him to experience this encounter. This is what I like to call "low hanging fruit." James had no doubt that the Lord was dealing with him. I asked him to wait a few minutes for me to retrieve my friend that I wanted them to meet. I really wanted the young disciple to have the experience he was looking for in his visit.

I brought him down, introduced them, and let them chat for a while. I actually went back up to the room and left them alone. It was not long before the young man returned quite distraught. You could see disappointment all over his face. I asked what had happened in their meeting.

He told me that James was right in asking him, "Do you really think you can come here to New Orleans and change a city, one person at time?" That really challenged the young disciple. It caused him to look away from whom he was ministering to and focus on the bigger picture of the whole city. We must always remember that Jesus most often ministered to individuals more than to crowds. Our goal is not to win cities but to impart life to people.

I hurriedly went back down to see if James was still there, and I was relieved to see that he had not left. I approached him, continued our conversation, and eventually invited him to return home with us to start a new life. It was obvious to all of us by the peculiar circumstances that the Lord had ordained our meeting and there had to be providential reasoning behind it all. At that time we just so happened to have a bunkhouse behind the church where I was the pastor. I was able to offer him a home and a church family.

We took James to the bus station and purchased a one-way ticket from New Orleans to Huntsville. The bus was leaving that afternoon. As James was boarding the bus to leave New Orleans, I shouted out to him, saying, "Hey, James, God just changed New Orleans one person at a time." He just smiled and nodded his head as if to say, "Yes, He sure did."

I have to tell you the rest of the story. James moved in and started to adapt to his new surroundings and church family, but every so often, he would just disappear. It would only be for an hour or so. Then it might be longer, but he would always reappear as if he was never gone. It was not an everyday experience, but it did start to happen more frequently, until one day he was gone and never did "reappear." Needless to say, this not only puzzled me, but it also troubled me. I really thought what the Lord had been doing in James' life was going to stick. It was now seemingly obvious that James was the one who was not going to *stick* around.

After a few months had passed, I came to my office one day and found a letter on my desk that had been addressed by hand to me. The return address was the Limestone Correctional Institute in Athens, Alabama. The name attached was James. My heart sank. I thought if he had only stuck around here, he could have lived a free life. Now what had he gotten himself into?

I was surprised as I read the letter. He first apologized for his erratic behavior of disappearing and reappearing. He then began to explain why. He had been hiding from the police. Every time he saw the police, he would disappear in fear, thinking they were looking for him. About once a week, the Sheriff's Deputies would park in the church parking lot to keep from just riding around. James thought they were staking him out. He then revealed that he had become homeless because he was running from the law for previous crimes he had committed, so out of paranoia he would "disappear."

One day, conviction set in through what he had been learning and because of a new relationship he had with Christ. He knew that if he was ever going to have a truly restored relationship with his family, he was going to have to go through proper steps to get restored. He quit running away and living in fear. He turned himself in to the proper authorities, knowing it would result in time spent in the state penitentiary. Needless to say, I was dumbfounded, but relieved, as well.

It does not stop there. He corresponded a few more times. He shared with me that he really missed his church family he had found with us. He prayed that somehow he could see us. It was the next day that he was walking in the courtyard that he turned to see the young man who was the drummer at our church. This young man was on one of his first days of working at the prison when James called out his name. The young drummer was a bit surprised to hear an immediate calling out of his name, but excited to see it was James. His prayer had been answered. That young man had just been hired the day before to work in the classrooms at the prison.

He who the Son sets free is free indeed!

The Other World

It was just another Friday morning and I was at the airport. This time I was blessed to have my daughter, Micah, along with me. We were going to London, Ontario, where I was scheduled to be ministering at a young adults' conference. Micah's dear friend, Sydney, lived there, and it was a great chance to for them to reconnect.

While we were waiting to board our flight, I noticed an elderly woman watching Micah and me interacting. Micah was nine years old at the time and very well behaved for her age. She was not doing anything out of the ordinary. She was just walking to and from the window to see what our plane looked like.

The woman watching us was well groomed. I would say she was somewhere between seventy-five and eighty years of age. She was wearing a full, tan-colored, polyester suit. The blouse was a cream color. She was wearing laced up walking shoes and tan stockings. Her hair was perfectly set, as I am sure it was everyday, and had been for many days prior. Okay, it is obvious I was watching her, too. She was pretty well dated by her appearance. I was starting to wonder if maybe she was somewhat disturbed by Micah's and my style. Maybe she was thinking I was a single parent and that Micah needed to be with her mother instead of this guy with an un-tucked button down shirt, pocket-designed jeans, and, to finish it all off, pointed shoes!

We were obviously worlds apart in our styles and appearances. I was really wondering what she might have been thinking about us. Then I noticed she was approaching me. "Wow! She is bold," I thought. She kindly and politely greeted me with a meek, "Excuse me, may I ask you a question?"

Having all my attention, I replied, "Yes, Ma'am." "I am curious as to where you bought your daughter's backpack. I find it very cute and think my granddaughter would like one." This was totally not what I was expecting. I was actually thinking she may be put off by our "relevant" apparel.

Micah's backpack was pink, the best I can remember. It had a stuffed animal, a monkey, that stuck in one of the pockets of the backpack. She was right. It was cute, but I had no clue as to where it had been purchased. I asked Micah, and she graciously told the woman where it could be found.

This opened a conversation, and I asked her where she was from since she had a strong European accent. She replied, "Hungary."

She quickly asked me where I was from and where I was flying to. Answering her, I mentioned I was in the ministry and that was why we were flying to Canada. Her response is one I will never forget. "That is nice. I used to have faith before my husband died, but that was in the other world."

I was stumped. I did not know what to say. There I was a traveling evangelist, meeting face-to-face with someone who says she "used to have faith." What caused her to lose it? Here was a woman who said she *used* to have faith before her husband died. Was she hurt in a church? Had she gotten mad at God because of her husband's death?

Obviously, that had something to do with it, or she would not have said anything about it. But isn't death all a part of life?

There is an appointed time to be born and a time to die, and it is the death that ushers us on to eternal life with Christ. This has always been something that amazes me. Everyone wants to go to heaven, but no one seems to want to die. I was stumped at her statement: "I used to have faith before my husband died, *in the other world.*" I had to draw on the Holy Spirit because I did not know what to say and especially did not know what she meant by "that was in the other world." Jesus said we will be given the words we need when we need them by the Holy Spirit.

All of a sudden, it hit me... the other world. She was a Holocaust survivor. She had lived through the Holocaust, but her husband must not have survived in "the other world." It was so terrible during those days, for not only Jews, but for the Christians who had harbored them. She was obviously one of the Christians involved in protecting Jews. She had lived through the torment, but her husband had not. It was there that she had lost her faith in God.

I must say, she was no heathen by nature. She was a very pleasant woman, of obvious integrity and wholesomeness. She was very polite and actually happy for my "faith" and for me. She was the first, and, to my knowledge, the only Holocaust survivor I had ever met in person. I was still in awe. There are not many left. That was one of the most horrific times in the history of the Jewish faith and for the Christians who gave them shelter and showed them any type of kindness. It was actually of biblical proportions, likened to the slaughtering of the Hebrew boys two and under in the time of Moses' birth, and the massacre of the boys two and under by Herod during the time Jesus was born. It was terrible!

Now, there I was, face-to-face with a survivor who had abandoned her faith. What was I to say? I actually had nothing to say at that moment. It was now time to board our plane to Detroit en route to Ontario. All I knew to do was help her with her baggage as we were starting to board, and she was grateful.

Our seats were at the very front of the plane. I was not certain as to where my elderly acquaintance was seated but I knew it was somewhere behind me. I could not get her off my mind. I knew I needed to spend some time in the Word and prayer as we flew, so I reached for my Bible. I would be preaching that night in a conference and would not have much time to prepare once we landed. The moment I opened my Bible, the Holy Spirit spoke to me, "Write her a love letter."

I knew exactly who He was talking about, but what on earth would I say to her? I was not only getting ready to prepare myself to preach, but I was trying to get my mind off of the woman from the other world. Now I had the Holy Spirit telling me to write her a love letter. Keep in mind, although the Holy Spirit was speaking to me, I was still having those carnal thought processes that are normal in everyday life, and they are such a hindrance to following the Spirit's leading.

My thoughts were something like this: first, love letters are for lovers, not strangers. Secondly, how on earth do you write a love letter to an eighty-something-year-old woman? (Not to mention one who has lost her husband and is from the "other world.") I knew what I needed to do. I needed to listen to the Holy Spirit; he had something He wanted to say to her. I just needed to let my pen write the words the Holy Spirit would give me.

I opened a note pad, took my pen, and just let it flow. I really cannot even remember what I started to say, but I remember full well what I finished in writing to her. I am pretty sure the beginning was something to the effect of being privileged and honored to have met her, and that I was terribly sympathetic regarding the loss of her husband. I am sure I wrote a few more things. It actually took me most of the flight. As I said, I know exactly how I finished the letter, and it did not seem to be the appropriate finish for an ordinary love letter.

It was not meant to be an ordinary love letter. This one was straight from the Holy Spirit. I finished by saying that I was sorry she had experienced such grief and pain, how she had suffered so much in the other world, and how it caused her to leave her faith. Albeit so foreign to me and hard to fathom or imagine, it did not change the truth of God's Word no matter how much she had suffered. For you to be forgiven, you must forgive others their sins, too. If you do not forgive others their sins, nor will or can your sins be forgiven. Although this comes straight from the Scriptures and quoting the teaching of Jesus, right after, He taught them the Lord's Prayer. That day it was coming straight from the Holy Spirit as I wrote.

She had obviously not forgiven those who had taken her husband's life and the One who did not keep him from dying, God Himself.

She had been living in unforgiveness all those years. She had forsaken God and held resentment toward Him for all that had happened in the other world. She had made a new life in America—a life of her own.

I folded the letter and told Micah I would be right back. I went toward the back, looking for her in the fully occupied plane. I did not reach her until the next-to-last row in the rear of the plane. She was fully engaged in conversation with the gentleman seated next to her. I politely interrupted and got her attention. I simply gave her the "love letter" and said the Lord wanted me to give this to her. She replied with a pleasant "Thank you." I returned to my seat in the front of the plane.

I was just in time to be seated for the flight attendant to inform us we were ready to prepare for our final descent—no more time to do anything but buckle up, lift my tray table and bring my seat forward. It was time to land.

As I said, we were in the very first seats on the plane, so we were the first ones off the plane. I never take much time exiting a plane, and getting to the baggage claim, and on to the rental car desk.

We had not gotten more than five or six gates down the concourse when I heard someone saying, "Sir, excuse me, sir." I turned around, and guess who it was? My dear friend from "the other world." How on earth she ever caught up with us is still a mystery—or should I say, a miracle—to this day. I must add, she was not even out of breath. The only way I can even begin to describe the wonder in it would be to liken it to Elijah out-running the chariot on foot!

You think I was stumped earlier? Now I was absolutely amazed! She was not panting for breath, but she had tears running down her face. And she said to me:

"Thank you, Sir. I have found my faith again."

There I stood, amazed at His grace once again—one saved through His grace by means of the prophetic voice, or in this case, prophetic writing. Yes, I was totally amazed!

72 11

I had been invited to minister at a youth conference in Hamptons, Virginia for a close friend of mine. This wasn't going to be just another youth conference. It was going to be a cutting edge event to set an atmosphere for youth to experience the presence of God in a tangible way. They were expecting a few thousand teens to attend the weekend conference. Not only was I going to be speaking at the youth conference, but he church had extended an invitation for me to minister in their two Sunday morning services. Needless to say I was excited about this weekend!

Knowing that this was going to be a great weekend I included the guys and girls who were in our discipleship program to come along. There was no way I wanted them to miss this experience. The expectation in my heart was very high and for good reason. The Conference Host is a dear friend of mine and I knew He wanted nothing less than a powerful move of God. He and I share the same passion to see the next generation set ablaze with a passion for His presence. Knowing this would be a great opportunity for the guys on our team to have a great corporate encounter with God. I also had them bring along my two oldest sons, who at that time, were around seven and eight years old.

The host had booked me a room at the Hampton Inn so it made perfect sense to book a few rooms at the same hotel for the team members who were traveling with me. I was thankful to find that my room was conveniently located on the first floor. Having not booked the rooms at the same time, the guy's rooms were on the second floor at the opposite end of the hall from where my room was. A couple of hours before the Friday night service I went down the hall and took the elevator up to the second floor. I wanted to spend some time with the team in prayer before the night session. Having finished a sweet time of prayer I was going back to my room to get ready for the conference. Instead of using the elevator as I had on my way to their room, I just felt the urge to walk down the hall to the stairwell and take the stairs down to the first floor as my room was right next the stairwell. As I was walking down the hall, about halfway, I suddenly heard voices in the room to my right. It was so startling that it stopped me dead in my tracks. It was clearly a domestic dispute between a husband and wife. It was also obvious that there was a young daughter in the room as well. She was crying and saying, "Please stop." The wife was trying to plead with the angry husband. He would have none of it, as his voice climbed with rage. I heard the woman respond in a way that it seemed he had physically addressed her in some way. I could actually hear the sound of a slap. The mother gasped with pain and shock, while the daughter reacted with a shrill cry and the desperate outburst of, "Mommy!" On any given day my first response would have been to knock on the door and raise my voice in a manner to get someone to the door. My after thought was that I should have just kicked the door down. (Not quite sure I could even do that, but the image in my mind tells me I could have done it with the best of any silver screen hero.) When it comes to a spirit led or prophetic evangelism lifestyle, we must always remember that our ways are not His ways. His ways are always higher than ours. Not only was I shocked by the commotion I was hearing in the room 211, I was totally taken off guard at my unhesitant response. I turned and ran toward the stairwell as fast as I could, taking two steps at a time to get down the stairs and reach the first floor. By the time I got to my room I already had my door key out and putting it into the door. All along the way I was thinking, "Why on earth am I running away from this situation?" Without a doubt I knew the Spirit was leading me, but I had no idea where He was taking me. It is one of those feelings that you are not sure if you love it or hate it. Sometimes the Holy Spirit will take you places you would have never taken yourself and it is not always green pastures and still waters. He will use those who will let Him take them to places where "death works in us so that life can work in others." He can lead you into some sketchy situations for the sole purpose to help lead others out of the darkness of deception and the snare of the devil. Reaching those who are in the hands and plans of the enemy can place you in the frontlines of the battlefield!

Many years ago I had a little saying that I thought was pretty cool. "I hate what I have to do, but I love the One for who I do it for." I did not get to say it too many times before the Lord responded, "Do not say that anymore. They are the same!" Doing it for Him and doing it to Him are one in the same. Obedience is what pleases the Lord and ministering unto the least of them is the same as doing it unto Him. So I have grown to learn to love that feeling!

As soon as I got into the room I sat down on the bed and picked up the phone receiver on the table between the two double beds. Without any hesitation I dialed **7211**. Why 7211? To reach another hotel room without having to going through the front desk you can add an extension to the room number and in most cases it is the prefix of the number 7. This would dial me straight to the room that I had just run away from. After two rings there was an answer. It was a harsh "Hello!" It was the voice of the man whom I had heard yelling at his wife and the daughter. Who most likely was the one who had just slapped the woman a few moments earlier. I had no time to think up what I was going to say to whoever answered the phone, in fact, I didn't even know I was going to be calling the room. Now what? Just as I had not given thought to knocking, kicking or running away from the room, the words just came out of my mouth, "I want you to know that Jesus loves you and your family. He wants to touch your life and heal all your wounds." The response from the other end of the receiver is a bit difficult to quote, but I will give it my best. He said, "Holy —!" And then I heard his body fall on the bed as if he just fell over. It was obvious to me that the power of God just swept over him. I could then hear the daughter say. "Mommy what just happened to daddy? Is he okay?" All the crying and screaming stopped in a moment. You could tell the violent spirit had left the room. The wife then picked up the receiver and said, "Who is this?" I just simply shared with her that Jesus was now stepping in to not only protect she and her daughter but that He was able to heal their wounds as well. She removed the phone from her mouth and said, "Honey it is going to be okay. Jesus is here." We never spoke another word, nor did we ever see each other in the hall or the lobby. It reminded me of the time in the ministry of Jesus where the lame man "looked up and saw no one save Jesus." May it be so with our ministry as well.

Go Call Your Wife

There are not many books I come across, that once I start reading them, I cannot put down. "*No Compromise,*" the life story of Keith Green, is one of those books. As a matter of fact, I read it twice back-to-back. During my second reading of the book, I took a brief trip back to New Orleans. Flying is always a great time to do some serious reading. I was really looking forward to getting some undisturbed reading time, or so I thought.

Unknown to me, the very weekend I was traveling into the city, there was a rowdy group of weekend party-goers also descending upon New Orleans. It was the annual Decadence Celebration. Decadence in New Orleans is where thousands of homosexuals come for the weekend and literally celebrate their pride in decadence. The atmosphere on the plane was anything but peaceful. I was certainly in the minority regarding sexual orientation.

Seated next to me, behind me, and in front of me were all gay men who evidently knew each other. They were not shy at all regarding their sexual preference. It was also obvious to them that I was not of the same preference. Their flight now seemed to be a mission to make me uncomfortable. Once I pulled out my book, the guy next to me made it known to all those around me. He obviously had some Christian background and some resentment toward Christianity. He made numerous comments regarding Keith Green and the "Christian's way."

Numerically, the odds were against me, and I was beginning to feel a good bit intimidated. I wanted to say something, but I knew it was my flesh. I wanted to put the book away, but I knew that was fear. It was the longest hour-and-a-half flight I have ever taken. I just wanted off the plane.

Once we landed, my goal was to get to my hotel as quickly as possible. Frustration had settled in, and I actually felt inadequate, insecure, unprepared, and unconcerned to be there at all. The next morning, I felt content to just sit in my room and read. It was mid- afternoon before I really sensed the Lord leading me to take a walk through the French Quarter. Not sure where or whom I would be ministering to, I just knew I needed to go. Jesus said that those who are who are born of the Spirit are like the wind. You do not know where it comes from or where it is going. So it is when we are led of the Spirit.

From the time that I set out, it was almost two hours before I knew I was where He wanted me to be. I was in front of the Royal Sonesta Hotel on Bourbon Street. I was facing Canal Street when I noticed seven men walking my way. They were obviously coming from a convention. Many corporations host the conventions in downtown New Orleans, using the nightlife to draw more attendees. That is what these men were looking for—nightlife.

Once I saw these guys, I literally zoned in on them. They had no idea whatsoever that I even existed. They were into their conversation, and I might add, it was loud. I could hear every word they were saying. The attractions around them had them captivated, as well. All seven of the businessmen had large cigars hanging out of their mouths. The size of the cigars matched the sound of their voices and the color of their personalities. I noticed that five of the men had on weddings bands. I meant it when I said I was zoned in on these guys.

They stopped right in front of me where I was standing on the sidewalk. Across the street from us was a gentlemen's club, or, in other words, a strip club. One of the men said out loud to all the guys, "Hey, why don't we get a room here, (pointing at the hotel behind me) in case we mess up over here tonight (pointing at the strip club)."

They all laughed.

This was another way of saying, "Let's get a room in case we get hooked up with a stripper. "It is important to note here that there is no distinction between sexual preference when it comes to sin. God is as displeased with un-natural affection as He is with sexual immorality and fornication. He is not a respecter of persons, but through Jesus Christ He has made atonement for our sins.

Right when the man made that statement, I had a strong unction to say something. I was no more than five to ten feet away from these guys. As much as I was in earshot of their voices, they, too, were in earshot of mine. I just knew I had to say something to them, after hearing what he had said, and hearing the response of the other guys, and seeing that five of them had on wedding rings (including the one who made the statement)! It came boldly to me to say:

Why don't you call your wives and see where they would want you to stay tonight?

You notice, that quote is not in quotations. I chickened out. I never said a word. I was worried about how they would respond. Would they get mad and retaliate, or tell me to mind my own business? I felt just like I had felt on the plane the night before. There was no doubt, I had given into the fear of rejection. I walked away and said nothing at all.

I walked briskly back to the hotel room, knowing I had just missed the Lord. As soon as I got in the room, I fell face first on the bed and wept. I was broken. I told the Lord I was sorry for giving into fear and for not obeying His voice. His response to me was, "Were you not willing to suffer the pain their wives may one day experience due to their husbands' behaviors?" His words to me were anything but comforting. It broke my heart more than I ever knew it could be broken.

You may be wondering why I am telling a story about missing the Lord. All the previous chapters have been to inspire and encourage you that it can be done. This chapter is meant to burden you that *it still needs to be done.* One main key to prophetic evangelism is that the prophetic is God's way of communicating to lost humanity by using a faithful human voice. Those who are living in sin cannot hear the voice of God.

"How then shall they call on Him in whom they have not believed? How shall they believe in Him in whom they have not heard? And how shall they hear without a preacher? And how shall they preach unless they are sent? As it is written;
How beautiful are the feet of those who preach the gospel of peace. Who bring glad tidings of good things!" (Rom. 10:14, 15) NKJV

All the Lord's People

It is my hopeful expectation that you have not only enjoyed these testimonies, but that you also have been inspired and encouraged to be used of the Lord in this manner. There are two ingredients needed for prophetic evangelism. Simply put, it is a blend of being prophetic and having an evangelistic heart or being evangelistic and having a prophetic edge. Most people wrestle with the idea of being prophetic. Many believe it is limited to only those who have the predetermined, God given, office of a prophet. There is no doubt that there are people who have been ordained from before their mother's womb to be a prophet, like Jeremiah. It is important to emphasize that being prophetic does not require one to be in the **office** of a prophet, but rather to have the **gift** of prophecy given by God.

Before we go any further about being prophetic it is most vital that a believer has an evangelistic heart. If someone does not have a heart for souls, I hesitate to believe whether he or she has the heart of God! To follow that, if someone does not have the heart of God, then the question rises, "Does God fully have their heart?" My persuasion is that all believers should have a heart for souls!

For God so loved the world that He gave His only begotten Son, that whoever believes in Him should not perish but have everlasting life. (John 3:16)

I am convinced that being born again results in having God's heart for souls just as I am convinced that we, as believers in the Lord Jesus Christ, and having the Spirit of the Living God dwelling in our hearts, each are meant to live a prophetic lifestyle to one extent or another. If you are looking for a more prophetic lifestyle that would result in reaching others for Christ, here are a few final thoughts that I have found to be critical to living a prophetic life.

First let's establish the heart of God regarding whether you can be prophetic or not. Take a look at what Moses said to a young servant and one of his choice men, Joshua in Numbers chapter 11.

²⁹ Then Moses said to him, "Are you zealous for my sake? Oh, <u>that all the LORD'S PEOPLE WERE PROPHETS</u> and that the <u>LORD WOULD PUT HIS SPIRIT UPON THEM</u>!"

Moses, at that point and time, was the one hearing and seeing God and speaking on behalf of God. He was the only one living a prophetic lifestyle. The burden of leading the people of God was becoming too great for Moses and he was going to need some help from people who would share in shouldering the burden.

We see here that God raises up a prophetic army out of those who will help carry the burden by placing His Spirit on them. The burden, in regards to prophetic evangelism, goes beyond someone simply repeating a prayer. This "burden" has the desire for people to encounter God in such a powerful way that it will drive them to hunger for hearing the voice of God for themselves.

God instructed Moses to select people he knew to be of proven character. They were to be officers to the people because they knew how to lead which was birthed from knowing how to follow. Being an officer also showed that they knew how to walk in authority correctly. The main reason they were given authority was because they had been submissive to authority. It is just like the Centurion soldier who recognized that Jesus was one who was **under** authority and that is what truly **gave** Him authority. Luke 7:8 This is exactly how we need to be when it comes to prophetic evangelism, doing what we hear our "Master" instruct us to do. Go, come, do this, do that....

Submission produces authority!

So, God is looking for people of proven character who will be obedient and submissive. Look at the word sub-mission. Sub means to come under, like a submarine or a sub-contractor. We become less and He becomes more. We simply come under His mission! That is what we are aiming to do...to learn how to minister like Jesus ministered. He only did what He saw and heard! He submitted to the mission God the Father had, to reconcile the lost world back to Himself.

God is looking for more people He can put His Spirit on and to influence them to touch the world for Him. He told Moses to gather these men of character and that He would come down and put His Spirit on them. Notice, God did not want to take the spirit of Moses and put it on them, but the same Spirit that He had placed upon Moses He wanted to put on those willing to bear the burden.

The Lord then had Moses to tell the people to "consecrate themselves" and watch for the "wonders" of God to happen. One of the most supportive roles to being prophetic is living a fasted lifestyle (consecration). This comes from choosing to live a life of self-denial, radical sacrifice, and spiritual disciplines that will help keep our eyes, ears and heart from growing dull to the voice of the Lord. He is not only the Lord of our lives but He is the Lord of the harvest (souls) as well.

Regrettably there seems to be so few laborers in the fields that He said are "white unto harvest."

The Lord also asked Moses, "Is My arm too short?" God is looking for a people who not only have a personal faith for their own salvation, but a faith that can believe for others that "all things are possible" through Christ our Lord. When it comes to being used prophetically there is not room for unstable faith. It is the prophetic that establishes faith in the salvation of the Lord. The prophetic also has the capability to enhance other's faith in the Lord Jesus just as is says in Roman 10:17

"Faith comes by hearing and hearing by the word of the God."

When people hear the word of God, (prophecy) it causes their measure of faith to be activated. When speaking prophetically it is important to be doing so without hesitation, doubt, or uncertainty. We must always speak and know that all things are possible with God. It is the purpose of the prophetic evangelist to build and establish the hearer's faith as stated in 1 Corinthians 14:3. Remember we are preaching the "good news" of the gospel.

Once again, Let's look at what Moses said to Joshua; "Do not be zealous for my sake..." This translates to, do not be envious on my account. Moses understood that it was not about the man of the hour with faith and power. The gifting and operations of the Holy Spirit are not to be reserved for an elite few, but rather, they are for His elect and chosen people! God is not a respecter of persons and it is His desire to pour out His Spirit upon all flesh, so that His sons and daughters shall prophesy... AND that as many as call upon the Lord, they will be saved.

Moses was the most humble (meek) man in all the earth. Jesus taught in the beatitudes that the meek would inherit the earth. It only makes sense that God had a plan to fulfill the desire of Moses when he said, ..."I would that *all* the Lord's people were prophets." We are earthen vessels destined to be bearers of the presence of God. We are a part of God's plan, which is to use a prophetic people to reach the lost. Like the apostle Paul asked, "Do you not know that your body is the temple of the Holy Ghost…?

When Moses said that he wanted all the Lord's people to be prophets, he was saying that he wished that all the Lord's people would hear God and speak on behalf of what they are hearing Him say! He also desired that the Lord would put His Spirit on them. We read in the book of Joel where he prophesies about the last days and that this is precisely what God is going to do. He is going to pour out His Spirit upon all flesh and His sons and daughters (all people) are going to prophesy. The end result is going to be that whoever shall call upon the Lord's name will be saved. Now if that is not prophetic evangelism, I do not know what is!

Here are my closing remarks for you. First, "Desire spiritual gifts and much rather that you will prophesy." 1 Corinthians 14:1 Secondly, make good choices and nominate yourself as a candidate that the Lord can use. Thirdly, Remember that Jesus said if we believe in Him we would do the same works that He did and greater works we would do. Many people have been called but only a few have chosen to follow Him in this prophetic lifestyle. He is looking for a few good men and women to fulfill His purpose of reconciling man unto Himself. His plan is to use those who can "hear and see" and will fully obey to reach those who have not yet tasted the heavenly gift and to bring them to the saving knowledge of Jesus Christ.

Remember the seven men in New Orleans? Five of which had on wedding bands. I missed it that time. And it still breaks my heart to think of the possible outcome their families may be facing because of my disobedience. There are still so many more out there that need that fresh prophetic encounter with the Living God through Spirit led prophetic evangelism.

Who is going to join the cause?

Will it be you?

This generation of Christians is responsible for this generation of souls.

Keith Green

Made in the USA
Lexington, KY
27 March 2014